OUT OF THE SHADOWS AND INTO THE LIGHT

OUT OF THE SHADOWS AND INTO THE LIGHT

The Exodus as a Pattern for Discipleship

W.J. Thomas, III

ELM HILL

A Division of
HarperCollins Christian Publishing

www.elmhillbooks.com

© 2020 W.J. Thomas, III

Out of the Shadows and into the Light
The Exodus as a Pattern for Discipleship

Published in Nashville, Tennessee, by Elm Hill, an imprint of Thomas Nelson. Elm Hill and Thomas Nelson are registered trademarks of HarperCollins Christian Publishing, Inc.

Clipart of Jesus carrying cross © Yuliya Nazaryan Nazaryan: www.dreamstime.com/jesus-carrying-cross-to-calvary-suffering-savior-image152573081

Elm Hill titles may be purchased in bulk for educational, business, fund-raising, or sales promotional use. For information, please e-mail SpecialMarkets@ThomasNelson.com.

Library of Congress Cataloging-in-Publication Data

Library of Congress Control Number: 2020903046

ISBN 978-1-400330584 (Paperback)
ISBN 978-1-400330591 (eBook)

❧ CONTENTS ❦

Dedicated to my wife,
Karen,
my greatest encourager during this project.
You are truly a Proverbs 31 woman.

⚭ ACKNOWLEDGMENTS ⚮

I am indebted to those who have partnered with me in this endeavor. Bob Crihfield and Jason Thomas gave early feedback. The Word Weavers group (Kent, Ohio), corrected many spelling and grammatical errors, as well as suggested more picturesque words to use. The team at Elm Hill gave detailed analysis and professional help. Most of all, I wish to thank the adult Bible school class I lead at Cornerstone Christian Church. They were the first to "field test" this material in a small group atmosphere, and afterward, they encouraged me to publish. It is a privilege to be with you each week.

෧ INTRODUCTION ෨

Shadowy Thinking:
Getting the Right Mindset

When I was in a full time preaching ministry, there were times when I struggled to know the direction I should proceed in my preaching, and there were times when God simply poured ideas into my lap. The skeleton of this book (the historical events and their corresponding spiritual meanings) came from one of those outpourings; I had to add the flesh on my own in the usual way. Rewriting those sermons in book format has caused me to take them to the gym to put some muscle on them.

I received these sermons on October 23, 2002 during a trip to the Cleveland Clinic. I was not looking for a series of sermons. I was not even in prayer at the time.

I was simply listening to a Christian radio station while accompanying a deacon of our church to one of his many radiation treatments for cancer. Sounds simple enough, doesn't it? But then they came! The information did not come verbally or in pictures, dreams, or visions. The best way to describe them would be joyous impressions. The more I meditated on each impression, the stronger the impression became. Within an hour, I had sketched out a six-week sermon series on the deliverance of the nation of Israel from Egypt through and including their settling in the Promised Land and the corresponding meanings in the New Testament.

I knew that I had received these promptings from the Holy Spirit. I also knew that I had the answer to a question that had bothered me for years. Months later, I preached this series and was again confirmed that it was of God. An unusual number of people remarked that the "spirit" of the services had been different. My prayer is that same spirit will come through these pages to you. Our study of this material will be through the use of "types and shadows," and its application will be in the area of Christian discipleship.

Types

The word "type" comes from the Greek word *tupos* and means "a die—i.e., a stamp or scar."[1] When looking at the word "type," one readily understands this is where the name was derived for the machine we call a typewriter.

I have a great deal of experience working in a factory that manufactures organ pipes for theaters and churches. One of the processes performed is to stamp identifying marks on each pipe, which leaves a designating impression in the pipe metal. In most cases, the impression is the exact opposite of the die. Many of the Old Testament types are similar to the strike and other types are the opposites. One quick example would be Adam as a type, an opposite, of Christ. "Nevertheless, death reigned from the time of Adam to the time of Moses, even over those who did not sin by breaking a command, as did Adam, who is a pattern of the one to come," Romans 5:14. Adam brought sin into the world; Jesus took it out. Adam brought death; Jesus brought life. Adam brought condemnation; Jesus brought justification.

Another word in this category I will occasionally use is "antitype." One might immediately think this is in opposition to the type because of the prefix "anti." *Anti* in Greek

---

[1] James Strong, *Exhaustive Concordance of the Bible with Expanded Greek-Hebrew Dictionary*, (Nashville: Regal Publishing), p. 73.

can mean "against" or "in place of." An antitype takes "the place of" a type because it is *the fulfillment* of the type. That which is full replaces that which is only partial. In the illustration used above, Adam was the *type* and Jesus was the *antitype*.

If you are unfamiliar with this method of Bible study, you might be asking yourself, "Is there any scriptural basis for this means of interpretation?" Yes, there is.

> For I do not want you to be ignorant of the fact, brothers and sisters, that *our ancestors* were all under the cloud and that they all passed through the sea. They were all baptized into Moses in the cloud and in the sea. They all ate the same spiritual food and drank the same spiritual drink; for they drank from the spiritual rock that accompanied them, and *that rock was Christ*. Nevertheless, God was not pleased with most of them; their bodies were scattered over the wilderness.
>
> Now these things occurred as *examples* to keep us from setting our hearts on evil things as they did....
>
> These things happened to them as *examples* and were written down as warnings *for us*, on whom the culmination of the ages has come.
>
> (1 Cor. 10:1–6, 11, italics mine)

This passage from the pen of the Apostle Paul establishes several important factors for our consideration. First, the *ancestors* that the Apostle Paul mentioned refer to the leaders of the nation of Israel during the period we will investigate. Second, there are several incidents mentioned within this text that show types (i.e., baptism into Moses, drank of a spiritual rock). Third, these things happened as *examples* to the readers and hearers of the epistle. The word used for the English *example* in Greek is *tupos*. Paul's purpose was to demonstrate that certain events happened to the Jewish people in time and space and in a real land with real people (historically), furthermore, these events have applications and lessons for his readers, and by extension, for us (spiritually). Chapter 3, "The Red Sea," will return to this passage.

Shadows

The other facet of our study will be through the use of *shadows*. Whenever light is cast upon an object, a shadow is formed. When one sees a shadow, he should be able to determine something about the object upon which the light has fallen. For example, the shadows of a dog, a man, or a tree should each be easily distinguished without having a degree in biology. Each shadow is definitive of its corresponding object, and yet none is a perfect representation. You may see the shadow of a man and still know very little about him. Is his hair red or brown? Is he married or single? Is he rich or poor? There are a thousand questions that cannot be answered unless you stop looking at the shadow and *look at the man*! God has cast his great light upon the truths of the New Testament and has caused their shadows to be formed in the events of the Old Testament. We will look at those Old Testament events (shadows) and their corresponding realities (substance).

Benjamin Keach, author of the voluminous *Preaching from the Types and Metaphors of the Bible*, had this to say about the shadows of the Bible:

> But where ceremonies and types of the Old Testament are called shadows with respect to Christ, Col. 2:17, Heb. 10:1; it is not to be understood that they are naturally so, but artificially, and like a picture, for painters first draw a shadow or an umbratile kind of delineation, and afterwards, perfect their picture with lively colours, the former vanishing out of sight.[2]

Mr. Keach compared a shadow to the outline of a picture that still needs the details filled in. That is precisely what this study will attempt to do. This survey will examine

---

[2] Benjamin Keach, *Preaching from the Types and Metaphors of the Bible*, (Grand Rapids: Kregel Publications, 1972) p. 105.

the shadows and types in the Old Testament Exodus story and then compare them to the realities behind each as found in the New Testament. What this form of study provides is the opportunity to see how YHWH,[3] *from the beginning*, had a plan for our salvation, and he used the nation of Israel to show that plan to the world.

Another passage that furthers our understanding of the use of *types* and *shadows* in interpretation is located in the book of Hebrews.

> Every high priest is appointed to offer both gifts and sacrifices, and so it was necessary for this one also to have something to offer. If he were on earth, he would not be a priest, for there are already priests who offer the gifts prescribed by the law. They serve at a sanctuary that is a copy and *shadow* of what is in heaven. This is why Moses was warned when he was about to build the tabernacle: "See to it that you make everything according to the *pattern* shown you on the mountain."
>
> (HEB. 8:3–5, ITALICS MINE)

The Book of Hebrews is steeped in picturesque language. Throughout its pages are found a multitude of

---

[3] Most often, when speaking of the Old Testament God the author will use YHWH, the tetragrammaton, instead of translating it as Lord, Jehovah, Yahweh, or God.

examples taken from the writings of the Old Testament. The author of Hebrews indicated at this juncture that the tabernacle was a "copy and shadow" (Heb. 8:5) of the realities which are in heaven. The Old Testament tabernacle was a shadow of the reality in heaven upon which YHWH's light had shined. The implication is this: *to better understand the unseen reality, look at the shadow which you can see.* In this passage, we see both of our words, shadow and type. "I don't see 'type,'" you might respond. But the Greek word *tupos* once again is here—this time, translated as "pattern" in verse 5.

Types and shadows are similar, yet different. They are similar in that each represents a New Testament (NT) truth displayed in part in the Old Testament (OT). They are different in that they each show a discernable pattern: types by the result of a blow, shadows by the casting of light. For our purpose, the terms will be used synonymously. The realities to which the types and shadows point are enlarged and enhanced from their original use. Using our illustration of Adam and Jesus above, once again: Adam was made in God's image; Jesus *is* God.

Some friends who prevued this introduction told me my explanations of types and shadows were confusing. If that is how you are feeling, let me simplify matters. When I was in elementary school, my teachers would occasionally pass out dot-to-dot pictures for us to complete. Types and shadows are like those pictures giving a glimpse of the picture that needed to be completed; most of the time, one could guess what the completed picture was even before it was finished.

In 2009, a motion picture was released entitled *Avatar*. Maybe you saw it. It grossed about $2.7 billion.[4] Change the aggressors in the movie to European colonists and the skin color of the Na'vi from blue to red, and *voila*, we have the American story of the settlers pushing the Native Americans across the continent for the sole purpose of garnering their land and its resources. Have you ever wondered how a nation founded on Christian principles could excuse such behavior? That question plagued me for years; *Avatar* brought it back in full force. Then one day I received the answer quite serendipitously. I was listening to a series of lectures by Robert Oden from *The Great Courses*® on the subject of "God and Mankind: Comparative Religions."[5] In the final lecture of the series, "Bringing It Back Home," he referenced a book entitled *The Puritan Origins of the American Self* by Sacvan

---

[4] Scott Mendelson, "Five Years Ago, 'Avatar' Grossed $2.7 Billion But Left No Pop Culture Footprint," December 14, 2014, https://www.forbes.com/sites/scottmendelson/2014/12/18/avatar-became-the-highest-grossing-film-of-all-time-while-leaving-no-pop-culture-footprint/#226641d66159.

[5] Prof. Robert Oden, *God and Mankind: Comparative Religions (The Great Courses*® on Tape), (Chantilly, VA: The Teaching Company, 1996).

Bercovitch. His explanation of the Puritan mindset gave me my answer.

> They (the European settlers) were not only spiritual Israelites…[s]ince they had migrated to another "holy land"…they conferred upon the continent they left and the ocean they crossed the literal-spiritual contours of Egypt…their enemies at home and abroad became more sinister Pharaohs.[6] (parenthesis mine)

The colonists were spiritual Israel who had escaped evil Pharaoh (England) and had crossed the Red Sea (Atlantic) to a new Holy Land (America). Who else could the Native Americans be than the Canaanites whom the historical nation of Israel was to annihilate or subjugate completely and take their land?

THAT, my dear reader, is typology gone awry. I hope I have avoided making such grievous interpretations within the confines of this work. You be the judge.

Here, now, is the premise upon which this book is written: YHWH purposely gave the people of the Old Testament types and shadows by which to better understand the coming New Testament. You might ask, "Why concentrate on these particular events? Why study the

---

[6] Sacvan Bercovitch, *The Puritan Origins of the American Self*, (New Haven, CT: Yale University Press, 1975), p. 113.

contours of the Exodus? Why do we want to look at that old story?" Why indeed.

Two reasons readily come to mind. First, it is my contention that the theme of the Exodus is the most referenced story in the Bible (see Appendix A). As N. T. Wright offered in 2011, "[The Israelites'] theme came to its fullest flowering in the great story of the Exodus…. Understand the Exodus, and you understand a good deal about Judaism. And about Jesus."[7] The exodus was a mighty act of YHWH that was meant to never be forgotten or neglected; hence, the celebration of the annual festival of Passover is still celebrated—even in our present time— in the Jewish community. Matt Proctor added, "In many ways, the story of the Exodus is the story of the whole Bible."[8] Finally, as Bryan Estelle has recently written:

Throughout the Old Testament, there are reminiscences of the exodus event again and again. The lexical, conceptual, and influential allusions to this founding event of the ancient Hebrew nation resonate throughout the Bible….[9]

[7] N. T. Wright, *Simply Jesus: A New Vision of Who He Was, What He Did, and Why He Matters*, (San Francisco: HarperOne, 2011) p. 33.

[8] Matt Proctor, *Victorious: A Devotional Study of Revelation*, (Joplin, MO: College Press, 2013), p. 95.

[9] Bryan D. Estelle, *Echoes of Exodus: Tracing Biblical Motif*, (Downers Grove, IL: IVP Academic, 2018) p. 1.

Second, the Exodus story and Israel's journey to the Promised Land is a picture of YHWH's plan of salvation and pattern of discipleship found today in the gospel of Jesus the Christ (Messiah). Allow the words of the late Victor Hoven to speak as well.

> [A] greater illustration of God's interest in humanity the Bible does not record. A race of helpless slaves, in the grip of one of the most powerful nations in antiquity, is delivered by the mighty arm of Jehovah through a series of wonders which shook the kingdom of Egypt to its foundation and published abroad his name among the nations. The means and manner of Israel's redemption, their subsequent history and destiny furnish the clearest conceivable understanding of the gospel plan of salvation through Christ, of the subsequent life and its meaning, and of the believer's eternal fortune and destiny.[10]

"A greater illustration of God's interest in humanity the Bible does not record" is a powerful and far reaching statement! Is it really that big? Yes, it is. The history of the exodus is repeated or alluded to over and over throughout the pages of Holy Writ (see Appendix A).

---

[10] Victor E. Hoven, M.A., B.D., D.D., *Shadow and Substance*, (Bloomington, MN: Bethany Press, 1934) p. 59.

Because of the number of references, we must understand this to be a major—if not *the* major—theme in scripture. The sequence of events in the historical narrative of the Israelites' journey is in the same order as the steps to maturity for the disciple of Jesus Christ. I hope this will become abundantly clear as exploration is made into each event.

It is my desire that this study will help one to see that from the beginning, YHWH had a plan to bring salvation and discipleship to the whole world. It will also clarify the details of the events as the New Testament *fulfillments* are brought into the light. This will be done by journeying with the nation of Israel from its bondage in Egypt to its warfare in the Promised Land. These events parallel certain spiritual principles in the life of every Christian. As we examine Israel's history, it will become evident that their struggles in history are the same struggles *every* believer has in their faith journey.

I invite you to travel along with the nation of Israel and consider their lives from slavery in Egypt to the entering into the Promised Land.

This book has been divided into three parts distributing the chapters between (1) the events that freed the Israelites from slavery, chapters one through three; (2) the events that brought them to the Promised Land, chapter four; and (3) the events that helped them to claim their promise, chapters five and six. The first division which we are about to scrutinize under the heading of "The Journey Out of Bondage" deals with the problems in Egypt, the initiation of the Passover, and the crossing of the Red Sea. I believe I have something to add to the traditional teachings where application is concerned. These first three chapters are a necessary foundation for understanding chapters four through six: covering the wilderness journey, crossing the Jordan River, and the entrance into the Promised Land. Those chapters will present a better understanding of the events than what has historically been presented. Alternative (and I believe, better) interpretations will be advanced to contrast the standard interpretations. Does the wilderness journey really represent the normal/average Christian life? Does crossing the Jordan River represent our crossing over in death? Does the Promised Land represent heaven? We shall see.

It is possible that this material will be used for study in a Sunday school class or a small group setting. To facilitate those purposes, a discussion guide has been provided in Appendix C. Several chapters can easily be divided into two studies. Chapters two through five each have explanations of the respective types and shadows and also an excursus.[11] The explanation can be one study and the excursus another.

My hope is this book will start conversations, not controversies; discussions, not divisions.

Enjoy.

W.J.T.3

---

[11] "An appendix or digression that contains further exposition of some point or topic." *Webster's New World Dictionary Second Edition*, (Cleveland: William Collins + World Publishing, 1974), p. 489.

PART ONE

THE JOURNEY OUT OF BONDAGE

CHAPTER 1

THE SLAVERY IN EGYPT

The Land of Bondage

During the summer of 2018, we had our garage reroofed—it was leaking terribly. I first discovered the problem when I found damp spots on my work bench. Upon opening my toolbox, I found my sockets swimming in a pool of water. They were all rusted. The water affected other tools as well. I have one pair of pliers I have yet to open—despite the application of large amounts of penetrating oil. They are so rusty I may never be able to use them again.

Rusty tools do not work well. This is true for the exegete of scripture as well. The Bible interpreter has a unique set of tools from which to select: history, grammar, culture,

word study, and the interpretation of types and shadows, to name a few. If you regularly delve into the scriptures, some of these *tools* may be quite familiar; others may have become rusty from disuse. One such apparatus is the use of types and shadows, which suffered after the Enlightenment. Bryan Estelle has observed in *Echoes of Exodus*, "In this book I will attempt to revivify a responsible use of typology, which has fallen out of favor in the academy."[12] I mention this, because it will be the primary method of interpretation used in this work. (For a fuller explanation of types and shadows, the reader is encouraged to see the *Introduction* of the current work.)

We begin this study in Egypt. Most people realize when a teacher talks about the Israelites (or Jews), the student expects the Israelites to be in or headed to the Promised Land. Their whole history revolves around God's promises to the Patriarchs, in particular, the Promised Land. So we must start in Egypt. But what were they doing there?

Even a cursory reading of the Book of *Genesis* will provide a list of references noting Egypt's long association with the nation of Israel. In fact, it went back to the time of the nation's progenitor, Abraham, or as he was called in his early years, Abram. "Now there was a famine in the land, and Abram went down to Egypt to live there for a while because the famine was severe" (Gen. 12:10).

---

[12] Estelle, p. 11

The early involvement of God's people with the Egyptians usually involved a famine striking the land in which the people of God were dwelling, with the result of God's chosen ones desiring to go to Egypt where there was food.

> Now there was a famine in the land—besides the earlier famine of Abraham's time—and Isaac went to Abimelek king of the Philistines in Gerar. The Lord appeared to Isaac and said, "Do not go down to Egypt; live in the land where I tell you to live."
> (GEN. 26:1–2)

When things got tough, Abram picked up and moved to Egypt. When his son tried to follow in his footsteps, YHWH[13] called a halt to it; he did not want his people in *that* land. Why did they want to go to Egypt? What was so attractive about Egypt? Why did they want to leave *the land* God had promised them on an oath? At least two reasons present themselves.

First, it was from a lack of faith. *Is God really going to meet my needs in the land where he has placed me?* And secondly, it showed a lack of tenacity for holding on to the promises of God. *Is this really the land God wants me*

---

[13] As was mentioned in the introduction, "Most often, when speaking of the Old Testament God the author will use YHWH, the tetragrammaton, instead of translating it as Lord, Jehovah, Yahweh, or God."

to have or is there another? Can I really survive here in this place or should I go to another?

We have all had doubts of these kinds. We can work multiplied hours in a local business or industry, but we never seem to get ahead. We just live from paycheck to paycheck. There appears to be a *famine* in the land. So what do we do? We start to look for a better place where we believe we can be prosperous—our economic Egypt. We also begin to doubt whether this is *the place* God wants us to be. After all, if God wants us here, shouldn't we be prospering above the "ungodly" with whom we are working?

This happens so easily. One looks around and notices those who are not serving God and yet…they seem to have greater blessings: they have the new cars; they have the Florida vacations; they have what we want! The temptation to not trust God creeps in. *If I cut back on my tithe or stop giving altogether, I can have those things too. God is not providing what I want.* It is time to flee to another place of business, another job, another church, another Egypt. Now, I realize holding down a particular job is not on the same level as holding on to the Promised Land, but the attitudes seems to be the same: lack of faith and lack of tenacity. When someone prayed for and was hired for a particular position, he praised God. Now, by their attitude and actions, they are saying they do not trust Him.

Goodbye old job; hello new job of God's new promise! If not, I will work it out on my own; I am so out of here!

Please notice, *in order to enter the land of Egypt, one has to leave the land of Canaan.* You cannot live in two worlds. Before anyone leaves one land for another, he or she should spend considerable time seeking God's input.

> If any of you lacks wisdom, you should ask God, who gives generously to all without finding fault, and it will be given to you. But when you ask, you must believe and not doubt, because the one who doubts is like a wave of the sea, blown and tossed by the wind. That person should not think he will receive anything from the Lord. Such a person is double-minded and unstable in all they do.
>
> (JAS. 1:5–8)

You cannot live in Egypt and in Canaan at the same time. You cannot live in the place of your choosing and the place of God's choosing at the same time; unless, of course, you both happen to make the same choice. You cannot live in the land of *doubt* and the land of *faith* at the same time. You cannot live in the land of Pharaoh and in the land of *promise* at the same time.

One might think, *Come on! What is so terrible about the land of Egypt?* Here is our first type, our first shadow. In the Bible, Egypt represents a place to have one's carnal appetite met, even though that appetite is outside the promises of God. *Egypt is a shadow picture of living a sinful lifestyle.* The historical Egypt was a nation of many gods and many idols; they were not serving YHWH. They were substituting other gods and idols in his place and ignoring him. So, if Egypt was so evil in the eyes of YHWH, why did the Israelites move there?

Moving to Egypt

We need a brief history lesson. Quickly recall how the nation of Israel found itself situated in the land of Egypt. Abraham (to whom the promise of the *land* was originally given) begat Isaac. Isaac begat Jacob and Esau. Jacob had twelve sons, his favorite being Joseph. Joseph—out of jealousy by his older brothers—was sold by his brothers to the Ishmaelites[14]/Midianites who then resold him into slavery in Egypt.[15] By God's design, he was elevated and became second in command; only the Pharaoh was higher.[16] Guess what happened next? Go ahead, guess!

Famine! That's right, another famine. One difference is this one affected Egypt as well as Canaan. The only reason

---

[14] Gen. 37:25

[15] Gen. 37:36

[16] Gen. 41:39–40

Egypt had "bread" was Joseph's wise administration of the previous seven years of plenty. This famine provided yet another opportunity for the people of God to go to Egypt and leave the land of Canaan. Joseph's brothers made several trips to Egypt to buy grain. Oh, they had not moved there, but their *association* with the land was deepening. On one of those "shopping trips," Joseph revealed himself to his brothers and was reconciled to them. Joseph, with the Pharaoh's permission, brought his whole family, seventy in all,[17] down to the land of Egypt where they settled in the area called Goshen. It seems, the Israelites came to Egypt in a very innocent (even a YHWH provided) way.

Most of us don't commit full-blown sin; we just dabble. We have poor associations. We don't start out doing anything wrong; we are just in the wrong place at the wrong time. Isn't that the way Satan often works? *Come over here for just a little while. It's okay to neglect God's promises for just a little while. You can always go back to them later.* Do you know how long the Israelites' "little while" lasted? Over 400 years![18] Those who moved to the land died in the land. The next generation born in the land died in the land. The next generation…well, you get the idea.

This history has been cited to flesh out two things: (1) what the land of Egypt represents from a spiritual

---

[17] Gen. 46:27; Ex. 1:5

[18] Gen. 15:13; "430" according to Exodus 12:40–41.

perspective—one's sin nature; and (2) how the Israelites wound up living outside of the Promised Land and living in the land of Egypt.

It all seemed so practical at the time! *We need food; Egypt has food. Joseph can procure food for us. We have been invited—with the approval of Pharaoh—to "come on down."* Sometimes our slide into a sinful situation seems harmless—even practical. How many of us have started something in a very innocent way with the best intentions, only to see the whole project fall to pieces? As the pastor of Christian churches for over twenty years, I have performed many weddings. I cannot recall even one couple who was not committed to make their marriage successful. Yet, many of those marriages did not last the test of time. They entered intentionally and were innocent of any wrong motive. Seemingly, they entered with good motives. Then something went terribly wrong.

It was the same for the nation of Israel.

Under New Management

Remember the unhappy employee who was looking for a new job? What often occurs with the change of a job (or a church) is we simply change one set of problems for another. We cannot see far enough down the road to know with any certainty the new job or new church will be better than the old job or old church, especially when change looms on the horizon.

After the Israelites had been in the land a long time, there was a change in management in Egypt—a big change!

> Then a new king, *who did not know about Joseph*, came to power in Egypt.
>
> So they put slave masters over them to oppress them with forced labor, and they built Pithom and Rameses as store cities for Pharaoh. But the more they were oppressed, the more they multiplied and spread; so the Egyptians came to dread the Israelites and worked them ruthlessly. They made their lives bitter with harsh labor in brick and mortar and with all kinds of work in the fields; in all their harsh labor the Egyptians used them ruthlessly.
>
> (Ex. 1:8, 11–14)

A king who did not know about Joseph? Where was he during history class? Many scholars believe there was a turnover in leadership because different people were in charge of the government. This Pharaoh was from another place; he hadn't heard of Joseph—therefore, he had no loyalty to Joseph's family. Here, the shadow of Egypt is refined: Egypt represents our life outside of our redemption in Christ, our life of sin. *It is hard bondage!*

Ponder how the events of the nation of Israel dwelling in Egypt are similar to the events that took place in the Garden of Eden. Do you remember how things were before the serpent showed up? Two innocent people just out for a stroll. Satan, *that snake*, showed up, and the next thing you know, Adam and Eve are strolling out of the garden! What started so innocently ended so tragically.

The Israelites had entered Egypt innocently enough, but now a strong brute, *a serpent in the throne*, had taken over.

If you think I am stretching things to put such a negative connotation on the land of Egypt, remember what the apostle and prophet John wrote in his revelation: "Their bodies will lie in the public square of the great city—which is figuratively called Sodom and *Egypt*—where also their Lord was crucified" (Rev. 11:8, italics mine). The two witnesses of God are slain and left in the street—like common carrion—for the birds to devour; a shameful act in any culture. This city "is figuratively called Sodom and Egypt." Let me help you. You do not want your name associated with Sodom! Why were these two names chosen to represent the city of Jerusalem ("where also their Lord was crucified")? Sodom represents the lowest *form* mankind can take in deviating from YHWH's plan; Egypt represents the *bondage* keeping mankind in slavery.

Even though they entered the land of Egypt in an

innocent way, they all suffered the same punishment, the same bondage. By the time YHWH delivered his people (about 400 years later), the ones he delivered had *all been born in Egypt.*

So also, when God comes to rescue us, we have all been *born in sin.* To restate what was written earlier: *The land of Egypt represents the bondage of the sin nature in every person.* After the first generation moved to Egypt, each person born thereafter was born in Egypt. And we, ever since the first generation of mankind sinned and moved out of the Garden of Eden, have been born in sin. This people of YHWH—these slaves to Pharaoh—did not have to *do* anything to be in Egypt; they were born there. We do not have to *do* anything to have sin attributed to us; we are born there. We have a sin nature. And what does the sin nature do? It keeps us in slavery! It keeps us in bondage!

> Don't you know that when you offer yourselves to someone as obedient slaves, you are slaves of the one you obey—whether you are slaves to sin, which leads to death, or to obedience, which leads to righteousness? But thanks be to God that, though you used to be slaves to sin, you have come to obey from your heart the pattern of teaching that has claimed

your allegiance. You have been set free from sin and have become slaves to righteousness.

(ROM. 6:16–18)

We are all born slaves of unrighteousness, but Christ has come so we can become his devoted servants—slaves if you will—to righteousness.

The New Boss

Not only are the Israelites in bondage, but look who is running the show in Egypt! The new Pharaoh. Here we find one more detail of the type of Egypt: *Pharaoh represents Satan.* Why do I believe that? Bryan Estelle has written, "Jesus' understanding of his own ministry primarily involved setting people free from the bondage and tyranny of Satan (who is the antitype of Pharaoh), releasing people from the slavery of sin, and announcing jubilee...."[19] Let's compare the Pharaoh to Satan.

Both Are Earthly Rulers

It is obvious to anyone who reads the Book of Exodus that Pharaoh was in charge of Egypt. He was an earthly ruler.

---

[19] Estelle, p. 245

His dominion and land mass could be measured. What about Satan?

> Again, the devil took him to a very high mountain and showed him all the kingdoms of the world and their splendor. "All this I will give you," he said, "if you will bow down and worship me."
>
> (MATT. 4:8–9)

The wilderness temptation of Christ—from which the above text has been extracted—is mentioned in all the synoptic gospels; it is mentioned in more detail in Matthew and Luke. One of the things about the interchange with Satan that has always amazed me is Jesus *never denies* Satan's authority of the kingdoms of the earth! He is the *ruler*. It is because Satan reigns in sin that Jesus had to come: "Since the children have flesh and blood, he too shared in their humanity so that by his death he might break the power of *him who holds the power of death—that is, the devil*" (Heb. 2:14, italics mine). Satan holds the power of death because he holds us in the bondage of sin. He constantly reminds us of our sin. He speaks words of hopelessness to us so we will not even *think* there might be one who could free us. Pharaoh bound the children of Israel in slavery and had complete control over their lives. He could kill them or he could let them live. The devil, through sin, has the same control over us. We need a bondage breaker—one who can defeat Pharaoh/Satan and deliver us to freedom.

Both Are Thieves

"Some people are like seed along the path, where the word is sown. As soon as they hear it, Satan comes and takes away the word that was sown in them" (Mk. 4:15). Satan steals the word of God, our hope of redemption. What did Pharaoh steal from the Israelites? Their freedom. They had moved into the land as free people, but because of Pharaoh's fear (Ex. 1:10), they were placed in bondage. I believe Satan also fears mankind. He fears we will worship God instead of him. He fears we will serve God instead of him. He fears we will join allegiance with God and fight against his kingdom. Therefore, he must keep us bound in our sin, and he must keep us ignorant of God. He must steal every opportunity to hear the word of God.

Both Are Murderers and Liars

Speaking to the Pharisees, Jesus said:

> "You belong to your father, the devil, and you want to carry out your father's desire. He was *a murderer* from the beginning, not holding to the truth, for

there is no truth in him. When he lies, he speaks his native language, for he is *a liar* and the father of lies."

(Jn. 8:44, italics mine)

In what manner was Pharaoh a murderer? In order to reduce the Israelite's population so they would not outnumber the Egyptians, all the baby boys were thrown into the Nile.[20] I realize the Pharaoh who did that was the father of the Pharaoh (possibly Ramesses II)[21] Moses later opposed, but he still acted in the office and power of the Pharaoh. It was his murderous threat that prompted Moses' mother to put him in a small ark among the reeds.[22]

And the Pharaoh Moses was in opposition to repeatedly *changed his mind.* He would tell Moses he could take the people and go, and then—as soon as the plague receded—he relented. That is a polite way of saying *he lied.* It is bad enough to do it once, but this Pharaoh lied to Moses (and YHWH) nine times! And even the tenth time, he changed his mind, and with chariots, pursued the Israelites.

---

[20] Ex. 1:22

[21] Ramesses II (1299–1232) is commonly considered to be the pharaoh of the Exodus by those who subscribe to the late date of the Exodus. (Unger 1988)

[22] Ex. 2:3

Both of Them Bind, Not Loose

We have already viewed verse 14 of Hebrews chapter 2, now let's read it again so we can view verse 15 in context:

> Since the children have flesh and blood, he too shared in their humanity so that by his death he might break the power of him who holds the power of death—that is, the devil—and free those *who all their lives were held in slavery by their fear of death.*
> (HEB. 2:14–15, ITALICS MINE)

Many people are afraid to die. I am not afraid of death, but I admit, the possible painful process concerns me. Many people, having been raised in a country where the gospel is freely preached, are afraid because they believe enough to worry—but not enough to repent. That reminds me of the old Blood, Sweat & Tears song "When I Die." Not only does Satan have the power to bind us through our fear, he can also bind us physically.

> On a Sabbath Jesus was teaching in one of the synagogues, and a woman was there who had been *crippled by a spirit for eighteen years.* She was bent over and could not straighten up at all....
> The Lord answered him, "You hypocrites! Doesn't each of you on the Sabbath untie his ox

or donkey from the stall and lead it out to give it water? Then should not this woman, a daughter of Abraham, whom *Satan has kept bound for eighteen long years*, be set free on the Sabbath day from what bound her?"

(Lk. 13:10–11 and 15–16, italics mine)

Jesus emphatically stated it was Satan who caused this crippling effect on this woman. Not disease. Not a terrible cart accident on the Via Maris. Satan. He is in the business of binding, not setting people free. In order to overcome Satan, Jesus promised the church the power to break his bondage. "I will give you the keys of the kingdom of heaven; whatever you bind on earth will be bound in heaven, and whatever you loose on earth will be loosed in heaven" (Matt. 16:19).

I am fully aware those words were spoken to Peter, not the twelve. But Peter, as the representative of the New Testament church, received those keys for all believers. To some extent (and I do not know the limitations of the extent, if any), the modern-day Christian church has been bequeathed those keys.

As Pharaoh repeatedly refused to release the Israelites, so also Satan refuses to let us go from under his power. He will do all he can to make us his subjects and to keep us under his rule. Make no mistake about it: *Satan wants you in bondage!* He will lie to you. He will promise you things he cannot deliver. He will keep you under his power—bound and hopeless.

If that is our end, what hope is there? How can anyone escape the grasp of such a powerful foe? It appears we need someone stronger than he is; we need a deliverer!

The Deliverer

As Moses was sent to set free the children of Israel, so also we have one who has been sent to set us free. *Moses is a shadow, a type of Jesus the Christ.*[23] Notice some of the similarities:

Both were miraculously preserved after birth.

Moses was saved from Pharaoh by the daughter of Pharaoh after he was hidden in an ark in the reeds (Ex. 2:5). Jesus was preserved from the wrath of Herod by going down to Egypt with Mary and Joseph after Joseph was warned by an angel in a dream (Matt. 2:13–14). In each case, the ruling power wanted to kill them; each acted out of fear of losing his grip on the leadership and loyalty of the people.

_____

[23] Keach, p. 976

Both gave up riches to become poor.

Having been found by and raised by Pharaoh's daughter, Moses made the difficult decision to *identify with* the poor, slave-bound Israelites rather than stay in the court of Pharaoh.

> By faith Moses, when he had grown up, refused to be known as the son of Pharaoh's daughter. He chose to be mistreated along with the people of God rather than to enjoy the fleeting pleasures of sin. He regarded disgrace for the sake of Christ as of greater value than the treasures of Egypt, because he was looking ahead to his reward.
>
> (HEB. 11:24–26)

And of course, Jesus left the riches of heaven to traverse this ball of dirt as one of us, a human. "For you know the grace of our Lord Jesus Christ, that though he was rich, yet for your sake he became poor, so that you through his poverty might become rich" (2 Cor. 8:9). "Since the children have flesh and blood, he too shared in their humanity so that by his death he might break the power of him who holds the power of death—that is, the devil..." (Heb. 2:14).

Your attitude should be the same as that of Christ Jesus:

> Who, being in very nature God,
>   did not consider equality with God some-
> thing to be used to his own advantage;
> rather, he made himself nothing,
>   by taking the very nature of a servant,
>   being made in human likeness.
> And being found in appearance as a man,
>   he humbled himself
>   by becoming obedient to death—
>   even death on a cross!
>
> (PHIL. 2:5–8)

Both were chosen and sent by God.

In Exodus chapter 3, we locate Moses being called and sent by YHWH who spoke out of the burning bush.

> When the Lord saw that he had gone over to look, God called to him from within the bush, "Moses! Moses!"
>
> (EX. 3:4)

"So now, go. I am sending you to Pharaoh to bring
my people the Israelites out of Egypt."

(Ex. 3:10)

"Now go; I will help you speak and will teach you
what to say."

(Ex. 4:12)

Not only was Moses chosen and sent by YHWH, he
also spoke only what YHWH told him to say: "Therefore,
say to the Israelites..." (Ex. 6:6). Moses did his best to
comply with YHWH's directives, but he ran into a stone
wall. "Moses reported this to the Israelites, but they did
not listen to him because of their discouragement and
harsh labor" (Ex. 6:9).

Earlier, we noted in Mark 4:15, Satan was a thief
who stole the word of God. He did this very thing to the
Israelites when Moses tried to share with them the good
news of their deliverance. Due to Pharaoh's suppression
of the people's spirits, they were unable to hear; they
were unable to believe. But Moses was told what to say
nonetheless.

Jesus was also chosen, sent, and given the words to
speak; and as we know, the people often would not receive
his teaching either.

(a) Jesus was chosen.

This was to fulfill what was spoken through the prophet Isaiah:

> "Here is my servant whom I have chosen,
>   the one I love, in whom I delight;
> I will put my Spirit on him,
>   and he will proclaim justice to the nations."
>
> (Matt. 12:17–18)

(b) Jesus was sent.

> "For God so loved the world that he gave his one and only Son, that whoever believes in him shall not perish but have eternal life. For God did not *send his Son* into the world to condemn the world, but to save the world through him."
>
> (Jn. 3:16–17, italics mine)

(c) Jesus was told what to say.

> "Don't you believe that I am in the Father, and that the Father is in me? The words I say to you I do not speak on my own authority. Rather, it is the Father, living in me, who is doing his work...."
>   "Anyone who does not love me will not obey my

teaching. These words you hear are not my own; they belong to the Father who sent me"

(Jn. 14:10, 24)

Both performed miracles by the power of God.

In most cases, Jesus' miracles were in direct opposition to Satan and his demons. As was noted earlier, Jesus healed the woman whom "Satan has kept bound for eighteen long years" (Lk. 13:16). Moses, likewise, faced off against the powers of darkness when, by his hand, YHWH sent ten plagues upon the land of Egypt. Moses' plagues were also aimed at Satan by picking off one idol after another.

> Do I mean then that food sacrificed to an idol is anything, or that an idol is anything? No, but *the sacrifices of pagans are offered to demons*, not to God, and I do not want you to be participants with demons.
>
> (1 Cor. 10:19–20, italics mine)

Egypt had many "gods" perceived to have varied powers over particular realms. Each plague was aimed at the realm of one "god." Each demonstration of YHWH had the purpose of removing one stronghold (one thing they depended on instead of YHWH) of sin in the Israelites' lives. Remember, the very ones Moses was trying to rescue had been born there, educated there, and enculturated there. They had been born apart from the knowledge and understanding of who YHWH is. They had been brought up in an atmosphere of idolatry; that was all they knew. Consequently, that ideology was manifested later when they cast a golden calf to be their god (Ex. 32:4).

This section was started with the caption "The Deliverer." That title was chosen because it speaks of Moses as the shadow of Jesus. What Moses did with the children of Israel in the natural realm, Christ has done for us in the spiritual realm.

Of Moses, Stephen, the first Christian martyr, spoke:

> "This is the same Moses whom they had rejected with the words, 'Who made you ruler and judge?' He was sent to be their *ruler and deliverer* by God himself, through the angel who appeared to him in the bush."
>
> (ACTS 7:35, ITALICS MINE)

And of Jesus, we read: "She will give birth to a son, and you are to give him the name Jesus, because he will save his people from their sins" (Matt 1:21).

The Greek word for "save" is *sozo*, which means "to save, i.e. deliver or protect."[24] Jesus saves us from our sins

---

[24] Strong, p. 70

by delivering us from the punishment we deserve—i.e., hell.

Moses was willing to give up the lucrative palace life to identify with his fellow Israelites (Heb. 11:24–26); Jesus gave up the riches of heaven and became a man (Phil. 2:6–7). Moses was the mediator of the old covenant, while Jesus is the mediator of a new and better covenant (Heb. 9:15).

Both had followers who were baptized into them.

The last parallel between Moses and Jesus is pertinent because they both had people who were baptized into their respective mission. We will cover this in detail in Chapter 3. But for now, let the following verses suffice: "They were all baptized into Moses in the cloud and in the sea" (1 Cor. 10:2). "Therefore go and make disciples of all nations, baptizing them in the name of the Father and of the Son and of the Holy Spirit…" (Matt. 28:19).

We have looked at the land of Egypt as a prophetic shadow picture of people apart from the message of salvation. We saw that Egypt represents: *(1) a place to have our carnal appetites met even though they are outside the promises of God; (2) our life outside of our redemption in Christ; (3) the sin nature of every person.* We have also seen within the larger picture the representations of Satan (Pharaoh) and Jesus Christ (Moses).

Discipleship Challenge

Like the Israelites in Egypt, we, too, have been held captive in bondage to sin from the moment of our birth. And the Lord has not left us without a deliver. Ours, though, is not a temporary Moses but an *eternal Jesus*. We can all receive deliverance from sin if we choose. In Jude 5, we find the following warning: "Though you already know all this, I want to remind you that the Lord…delivered his people out of Egypt, but later destroyed those who did not believe" (Jud. 1:5).

We serve a loving God who wants to see us delivered from our state of sin and bondage, but we also serve a just God who cannot allow sin to go unpunished. God's plan is to deliver those of faith and to destroy those who refuse to believe.

What will you choose today: deliverance or destruction…life or death…freedom or bondage? Are you willing, today, to acknowledge the sin nature with which you were born and repent of the resultant sin? Now that you understand the origin of your sin and the outcome of remaining in it, what will you do?

CHAPTER 2

THE PASSOVER

An Escape from Death

The old adage still stands, "You cannot judge a book by its cover." Then there is, "Beauty is only skin deep." If you have any doubts about that one, just check out the destructive relationships in the "beauty capital" of the United States—Hollywood!

As we continue our journey into the *shadows* of the life of the nation of Israel, let us not be caught up in surface appearances only. God has provided pertinent details for a reason. In this chapter, we are going to look at what is probably the best known *type or shadow* in the Old Testament—the Passover. It is delineated for us in the Book of Exodus.

The Lord said to Moses and Aaron in Egypt, "This month is to be for you the first month, the first month of your year. Tell the whole community of Israel that on the tenth day of this month each man is to take a lamb for his family, one for each household. If any household is too small for a whole lamb, they must share one with their nearest neighbor, having taken into account the number of people there are. You are to determine the amount of lamb needed in accordance with what each person will eat. The animals you choose must be year-old males without defect, and you may take them from the sheep or the goats. Take care of them until the fourteenth day of the month, when all the members of the community of Israel must slaughter them at twilight. Then they are to take some of the blood and put it on the sides and tops of the doorframes of the houses where they eat the lambs. That same night they are to eat the meat roasted over the fire, along with bitter herbs, and bread made without yeast. Do not eat the meat raw or cooked in water, but roast it over the fire—head, legs and inner parts. Do not leave any of it till morning; if some is left till morning, you must burn it. This is how you are to eat it: with your cloak tucked into your belt, your sandals on your feet and your staff in your hand. Eat it in haste; it is the Lord's Passover.

"On that same night I will pass through Egypt and strike down every firstborn of both people and animals, and I will bring judgment on all the gods of Egypt. I am the Lord. The blood will be a sign for you on the houses where you are, and when I see the blood, I will pass over you. No destructive plague will touch you when I strike Egypt.

"This is a day you are to commemorate; for the generations to come you shall celebrate it as a festival to the Lord—a lasting ordinance. For seven days you are to eat bread made without yeast. On the first day remove the yeast from your houses, for whoever eats anything with yeast in it from the first day through the seventh must be cut off from Israel. On the first day hold a sacred assembly, and another one on the seventh day. Do no work at all on these days, except to prepare food for everyone to eat; that is all you may do.

"Celebrate the Feast of Unleavened Bread, because it was on this very day that I brought your divisions out of Egypt. Celebrate this day as a lasting ordinance for the generations to come. In the first month you are to eat bread made without yeast, from the evening of the fourteenth day until the evening of the twenty-first day. For seven days no yeast is to be found in your houses. And anyone, whether foreigner or native-born, who eats anything with yeast in it must be cut off from the community of Israel. Eat nothing made with yeast. Wherever you live, you must eat unleavened bread."

(Ex. 12:1–20)

The institution of the Passover can best be understood by observing it in three dimensions:

- the *Passover policies* which deal with the *regulations* of the celebration
- the *Passover promises* which show the *benefits* of the celebration, and
- the *Passover participants* which detail *who* may partake of the celebration meal.

The Passover Policies

According to the Book of Exodus, the first nine plagues affected only the Egyptians[25] (this is a *type*—as discussed in the "Introduction"—of showing God's power over the strongholds of sin in our lives), but the last plague affected *all* who were in Egypt, because *all* needed redeemed.

This event in the history of Israel will demonstrate *the Passover is a shadow of our personal redemption.* The

---

[25] This is specifically mentioned in Exodus 8:22; 9:4, 22; 10:23.

following are the regulations God assigned to the Israelites to celebrate the meal in the proper manner.

First, he established *when* it should be celebrated. "This month is to be for you the first month…" (Ex. 12:2). As God prepared to do a new work in their lives, he gave them a new start in time, a new calendar. Their new start as a nation apart from their slavery in Egypt was the beginning of their first year of freedom. Whenever God wants to do a *new* work in you he will do the same thing. He will restart the clock. He will designate a new time as the point of your beginning. Could it be this is one reason we enter the life of faith through a *new birth*?

On most applications, space is provided for your birth date. Birth dates are important to the government and they should be important to us. In the first church where I was the preacher, a gentleman was honored with a surprise birthday party for reaching his eightieth year. We celebrated with him, and he reminisced over the goodness of God. We should do the same with our spiritual birth.

We need to take time, even mark time by dating our lives in Christ from our new birth. For a short time in our family, we practiced the tradition of having *spiritual birthday* celebrations. We gave Christian-oriented gifts (such as Bibles, books, music, T-shirts, and jewelry) on the anniversary date of the person's conversion. We looked back. We marked the day. We remembered. (I suppose we ceased celebrating out of laziness, busyness, or possibly economics.) Isn't having a new beginning an essential teaching of the New Testament?

> Jesus replied, "Very truly I tell you, no one can see the kingdom of God unless they are born again."
>
> (JN. 3:3)

> Jesus answered, "Very truly I tell you, no one can enter the kingdom of God unless they are born of water and the Spirit. Flesh gives birth to flesh, but the Spirit gives birth to spirit. You should not be surprised at my saying, "You must be born again." The wind blows wherever it pleases. You hear its sound, but you cannot tell where it comes from or where it is going. So it is with everyone born of the Spirit."
>
> (JN. 3:5–8)

"Therefore, if anyone is in Christ, the new creation has come: The old has gone, the new is here!" (2 Cor. 5:17). The Israelites needed a new start; so do we.

Second, on the tenth day of the month, they were to *select a lamb* (Ex. 12:3). Can you imagine the logistics of completing such a task? Each family would have to carefully inspect each of their lambs in order to determine if (1) it was the right animal (Ex. 12:3, 5); (2) it was the right size (Ex. 12:4); (3) it was the right age (Ex. 12:5); and (4) it was without defect (Ex. 12:5). Those stipulations sound very tedious and time consuming. Speaking of tedious, I have occasionally gone shopping with my wife. I can tell you from experience finding the perfect blouse is often an exercise in futility! "White blouse" is not very definitive. I really have no idea what she wants. On the other hand, God provided us with *many details*. Why did God spend so much time presenting what the attributes of the lamb should be? Because the lamb is a *type* of which Jesus Christ is the *antitype*. The apostle John mentioned this attribute of Jesus on two different occasions: "The next day John saw Jesus coming toward him and said, 'Look, the Lamb of God, who takes away the sin of the world!'" (Jn. 1:29). "Then I saw a Lamb, looking as if it had been slain, standing in the center of the throne, encircled by the four living creatures and the elders" (Rev. 5:6). As the Israelites had to inspect their lambs to make sure they met God's standard, we need to inspect the scriptures (both OT and NT) to make sure Jesus meets God's standard for the Messiah. Have you ever done that? Have you—at any time since you came to faith—personally studied to discover if Jesus is who the church says he is, or are you just accepting the word of someone else? We will make such an examination in an excursus below.

Third, after selecting a perfect lamb, it was kept

separate from the rest of the flock for a period of four days (Ex. 12:4a). This was to prevent it from being butted or injured, and thereby making it no longer flawless. The writer of Hebrews drew a parallel to this as well, "For we do not have a high priest who is unable to empathize with our weaknesses, but we have one who has been tempted in every way, just as we are—yet he did not sin" (Heb. 4:15). Jesus was flawless.

Then fourth, on the fourteenth day of the first month, the lamb was to be slain (Ex. 12:6). It is remarkable how this perfectly fits into the pattern of Jesus. Did I mention *the Passover lamb is a shadow of Jesus Christ*? As Peter wrote:

> For you know that it was not with perishable things such as silver or gold that you were redeemed from the empty way of life handed down to you from your ancestors, but with the precious blood of Christ, a lamb without blemish or defect.
>
> (1 PET. 1:18–19)

"Get rid of the old yeast, so that you may be a new unleavened batch—as you really are. For Christ, *our Passover lamb*, has been sacrificed" (1 Cor. 5:7, italics mine). As the Passover lamb was to be slain at twilight (Ex. 12:6) so it could be roasted and eaten that night, Jesus was slain (gave up his spirit) about three o'clock in the afternoon, so he could be in the grave before sundown.

The fifth policy they must complete, at least for the participants of the original Passover, was "to take some of the blood and put it on the sides and tops of the doorframes of the houses where they eat the lambs" (Ex. 12:7). Please note: it is not sufficient just to select a lamb. It is not enough just to keep the lamb apart for four days. It isn't even adequate just to slay the lamb. *The blood of the lamb must be applied* to the doorposts by faith! By doing this last part, the Israelites were saved from death. We, too, are saved by applying the blood of the Lamb to *the doorposts* of our hearts by faith.

I don't know if you have ever mused upon it or not, but blood is a status marker. It changes one's status:

- from sinner to forgiven
- from common to holy
- from dead to alive

Normally, just one of those markers is present. In the OT, when a blood sacrifice was offered, oftentimes its purpose was to remove sin (Lev. 16:15). Other times it was offered for making the common holy (Heb. 9:21–22). And lastly, during the first Passover, it kept those who applied the blood to their doorposts alive—changing their status from death to life. In Jesus the Christ, our Passover Lamb (1 Cor. 5:7), we have been given all three of these statuses because of his sacrificial death and free offering of his blood.

How does that happen? How does the shedding of a lamb's blood bring life? Later in the instructions to the nation of Israel, they would be given this command from God:

> "…any Israelite or any foreigner residing among them who eats blood, and will cut them off from the people. For the life of a creature is in the blood, and I have given it to you to make atonement for yourselves on the altar; it is the blood that makes atonement for one's life."
>
> (Lev. 17:10–11)

When a lamb's blood is shed, it literally gives its life—"the life of a creature is in the blood." If the blood is shed as an atonement, the lamb is giving his life for the life of the petitioner of God—a life given for a life. Therefore, when Jesus gave his life, shed his blood on a cross, he was giving his life for the one who comes to God in faith—a life given for a life. When one applies the blood of Jesus *by faith to the doorposts of his or her heart*, they receive life. But in what way are they given life? How does shed blood provide life? How does the transfer happen? I believe we have a clue in the writings of the apostle Paul: "Therefore, there is now no condemnation for those who are in Christ Jesus, because through Christ Jesus the law of the *Spirit who gives life* has set you free from the law of sin and death" (Rom. 8:1–2, italics mine). Paul also stated later: "He has made us competent as ministers of a new covenant—not of the letter but of the Spirit; for the letter kills, but the Spirit gives life" (2 Cor. 3:6). It seems the transfer bringing us life is through the Holy Spirit. In a manner of speaking, a mother gives her own life so her child can be born and have life. Could it be the Holy Spirit births us like a mother? When we are born again (Jn. 3:3, 7; 1 Pet. 1:23), we receive the sacrificial life of Jesus! This is how believers receive life from the blood of the Lamb.

Another requirement—the sixth—was to "eat the meat roasted over the fire" (Ex. 12:8). This aspect represents Jesus' total commitment to the cause. The sacrifice also represents our total participation and identification with Christ's suffering. As Jesus told his followers in another venue:

Jesus said to them, "Very truly I tell you, unless you eat the flesh of the Son of Man and drink his blood, you have no life in you. Whoever eats my flesh and drinks my blood has eternal life, and I will raise them up at the last day. For my flesh is real food and my blood is real drink. Whoever eats my flesh and drinks my blood remains in me, and I in them."

(Jn. 6:53–56)

It is ludicrous to believe, as many of Jesus' listeners did, he was calling them to be cannibals. He was calling them to total participation with him in his suffering and ministry.

> "Anyone who loves their father or mother more than me is not worthy of me; anyone who loves their son or daughter more than me is not worthy of me. Whoever does not take up their cross and follow me is not worthy of me. Whoever finds their life will lose it, and whoever loses their life for my sake will find it."
>
> (MATT. 10:37–39)

His call is the same today. He doesn't want us to taste but to be fully fed on him, "the bread of life." Speaking of bread...

Lastly, they were to remove all leaven (yeast) from the house and eat unleavened bread for one week (Ex. 12:15). The reason for this was because leaven was *a type* of sin (Matt. 6:6, 11–12; Mk. 8:15; Lk. 12:1). God wanted the community to live sin-free during this celebration. He especially wanted them to love God and love their fellow man (neighbor) as themselves.

> Get rid of the old yeast, so that you may be a new unleavened batch—as you really are. For Christ,

our Passover lamb, has been sacrificed. Therefore let us keep the Festival, not with the old bread leavened with malice and wickedness, but with the unleavened bread of sincerity and truth.

(1 Cor. 5:7–8)

It is not sufficient for one to just participate in this feast or *any* feast! God wants his followers to learn to celebrate together while acknowledging one another. They must celebrate with "sincerity and truth." Since the Passover feast is also *a shadow* of the Lord's Supper, one should pay attention to the words of Paul:

In the following directives I have no praise for you, for your meetings do more harm than good. In the first place, I hear that when you come together as a church, there are divisions among you, and to some extent I believe it. No doubt there have to be differences among you to show which of you have God's approval. So then, when you come together, it is not the Lord's Supper you eat, for when you are eating, some of you go ahead with your own private suppers. As a result, one person remains hungry and another gets drunk. Don't you have homes to eat and drink in? Or do you despise the church of God by humiliating those who have nothing? What shall I say to you? Shall I praise you for? Certainly not in this matter!

(1 COR. 11:17–22)

Though the Passover policies demanded the bulk of our attention, we still need to view the Passover promises and participants.

The Passover Promises

We now turn our attention to the Passover promises, which deal with the hopes of mankind. The first promise was immediate: "The blood will be a sign for you on the houses where you are, and when I see the blood, I will pass over you. No destructive plague will touch you when I strike Egypt" (Ex. 12:13). Get the picture? When one applied the blood of the lamb, he was saved from death and destruction; in a manner of speaking, *he received life*. He was saved from the plague which would come upon the rest of the nation. This was God's promise. As was noted in Chapter 1, the nation of Egypt represents our sin nature—our life outside of Christ. Therefore, everyone today also needs to apply this blood, because we are all under sin (Rom 3:23). We are not required to apply the blood to literal doorposts, but to the doorposts of our hearts.

The blood was applied over the door of each house. This was an *individual* application, an individual decision, not a national one (like the Day of Atonement which they were later commanded to celebrate). Each family had to express enough faith to select a lamb, kill the lamb, and put the blood of the lamb on their door frames. Today, each individual with the sentence of death hanging over his or her head (that is all of us) must apply the blood of *the* Passover Lamb, Jesus, to their hearts. This is mandatory to have life!

Do you realize what marking the door of the home would have done? The blood would be visible to the "death angel" and to fellow believers but also to the Egyptian soldiers and taskmasters, the followers of Pharaoh. We do the same thing when we apply the *blood of the Lamb* to our hearts: we are marked out to God, to fellow believers, and to Satan's hordes. When one surrenders his or her life to Jesus Christ—and he gives him/her a new life because of the blood—people will notice. Some will be glad and some will be mad. The redeemed in Christ will rejoice with the penitent believer. But there are groups of people in the United States whose purpose is to eliminate Christ's church—we are marked out as their enemies. Every time we participate in the Lord's Supper, it is a testimony to God, to ourselves, and to the unbelieving world we are a congregation of individuals who have applied the blood.

"For whenever you eat this bread and drink this cup, you proclaim the Lord's death until he comes" (1 Cor. 11:26).

Second, God not only promised life to those who, by faith, applied the blood, he also promised a *future*. Consider the following verse: "When you enter the land that the Lord will give you as he promised, observe this ceremony" (Ex. 12:25).

In the midst of detailing the Passover policies, he made a promise. He did not say *if* but *when*! "When you enter the land…" God was assuring them it was a done deal; they could bet their lives on it (come to think of it, they did). The two promises go together. Without life you have no future; with life you have a future. God was so sure of their release he told them *ahead of time* to plunder the Egyptians as they left the country.

> The Israelites did as Moses instructed and asked the Egyptians for articles of silver and gold and for clothing. The Lord had made the Egyptians favorably disposed toward the people, and they gave them what they asked for; so they plundered the Egyptians.
>
> (Ex. 12:35–36)

Think about this logically, you don't need goods if you are not going anywhere! You don't need plunder if your destiny is to be six feet under! God instructed them to plunder the Egyptians with two purposes in mind: to provide for the Israelite people, and to provide the materials for the house of worship—i.e., the tabernacle. Later in the Book of Exodus, Moses instructed the people to build the tabernacle. The people brought so much stuff (gold, silver, bronze, precious stones, and cloth) Moses had to restrain their giving! (Ex. 36:4-7). It was too much! In over twenty years of local ministry, I don't ever recall having that particular problem.

The people's complaints to God did not redeem them. Moses' many petitions to Pharaoh did not secure their release. No. God, not man, chose how to redeem. They were not released from Pharaoh (who, again, represents Satan) until *the blood was applied*. It broke him!

> During the night Pharaoh summoned Moses and Aaron and said, "Up! Leave my people, you and the Israelites! Go, worship the Lord as you have requested. Take your flocks and herds, as you have said, and go. And also bless me."
>
> (Ex. 12:31–32)

As Pharaoh was powerless against the power of God, so also Satan is powerless against the power of the blood. The blood is our *only* plea, our *only* source, our *only* hope for redemption from sin. It is our only resource for life and a future.

One last thought about the blood. Try to hold back your strong urge to cry out "Heretic!" *The blood does not seem to be sufficient for every need.* Hear me out. The blood was sufficient to preserve the lives of the faithful Israelites; it was sufficient to break the power of Pharaoh, but it did not separate them from their bondage. Though the blood was applied, they were still in slavery in Egypt. *It appears something else was needed.* What could it be? We will revisit this thought in the next chapter.

We still have one more aspect to investigate.

The Passover Participants

As much as God desires for all men to be saved, and as much as he wanted everyone in Egypt to accept his terms and apply the blood, there were certain *restrictions* regarding who could participate in the feast. "The Lord said to Moses and Aaron, 'These are the regulations for the Passover meal: 'No foreigner may eat it. Any slave you have bought may eat it after you have circumcised him...'" (Ex. 12:43–44).

No foreigner is to eat of it. We all understand the term *foreigner* in the natural sense. We might say it like this, "Anyone who is not a citizen." Who was the foreigner of whom God spoke? A foreigner was one who did not understand and submit to the *Initiator* of the feast—i.e.,

YHWH. Most of the Egyptians would have been disqualified because of this stipulation. God wanted to bring into close fellowship only those who had come to *know Him.* For someone to celebrate this feast without recognizing the God of the feast would have been to "eat and drink judgment on themselves" (1 Cor. 11:29). The Passover feast of the Israelites has morphed into the communion celebration of the Christians. No foreigner—i.e., no unbeliever—is allowed to participate. To ensure this, some churches practice "closed communion" where only members of that body may participate. It is better not to eat than to eat and be judged! (1 Cor. 11:29–30).

There is a second restriction mentioned in the verses above. In order to be a participant of the Passover meal celebration, the person had to be *circumcised.* Circumcision was a sign one had submitted to the Jewish faith and the Jewish God. All males were required to be circumcised or they were not allowed to be part of the covenant people (Gen. 17:14). What God established in Exodus 12 was a reminder of the covenant he had made with their patriarch, Abraham. Therefore, neither the Israelites nor those who joined their ranks (Ex. 12:44) could participate unless they had been circumcised in the flesh. The antitype to this is: neither can we participate in the Lord's table unless circumcised in the heart through repentance initiated by the Spirit.

Circumcision is a type of repentance. Though circumcision is sometimes compared to water baptism in the New Testament (Col. 2:11–12), here, the thought is repentance.

> Circumcision has value if you observe the law, but if you break the law, you have become as though you had not been circumcised. So then, if those who are not circumcised keep the law's requirements, will they not be regarded as though they were circumcised? The one who is not circumcised physically and yet obeys the law will condemn you who, even though you have the written code and circumcision, are a lawbreaker.
>
> A person is not a Jew who is one only outwardly, nor is circumcision merely outward and physical. No, a person is a Jew who is one inwardly; and circumcision is *circumcision of the heart, by the Spirit,* not by the written code. Such a person's praise is not from other people, but from God.
>
> (ROM. 2:25–29, ITALICS MINE)

The Holy Spirit circumcises the heart so one can receive Jesus Christ as Lord and Savior. It is one of those mysteries of the faith where the action of man (repentance) and the action of God (heart circumcision) go hand-in-hand.

Why would God concern Himself with circumcision of the heart? I do not mean to be insensitive to the reader, but have you ever thought about what happens at the moment of circumcision? The male reproductive organ contains one of the most sensitive places on his body—the very "top" of the penis. When a child is born, that part is covered with skin, making it less sensitive to its surroundings. By the removal of the foreskin, the most sensitive part of the penis is exposed.

This is a picture of what God wants from us in the spiritual realm. He wants us to cut away anything desensitizing our hearts toward him: attitudes, sin, and worldliness. He wants us to remove them through the process we call repentance. Cut them off and throw them away! Then we will be in the proper posture to approach his banquet table and participate in his feast in a sensitive way.

Excursus

We have stated Jesus is the Lamb of God, but did Jesus fulfill the policies of the Passover Lamb? I believe the policies making up this shadow need to be understood in a very nontraditional way. What I mean is this: *If Jesus is the fulfillment of these policies—and he is—then he must do so in every reasonable detail.* In order to receive this teaching, you will have to temporarily set aside the historical teaching of the church. My claim is not unique; I once heard a well-known radio Bible teacher say something similar.

On the tenth day of the first month, the lamb was set apart; and on the fourteenth day, it was slain. We know Jesus was slain, but in what way was he selected and set apart? Judge for yourself whether or not the following is true to scripture. I believe the year Jesus died, the tenth of the month (selection day) was on Sunday. Why? As Jesus came riding into Jerusalem on a donkey, the people cheered, shouted, and waved palm branches. They were *selecting him* as their king. They were recognizing him as the Messiah. In no other instance of holy week was there ever a popular recognition of him. The old sage Matthew Henry put it this way:

> All the four evangelists take notice of this passage of Christ's riding in triumph into Jerusalem, five days before his death. The Passover was on the fourteenth day of the month, and this was the tenth; on which day the law appointed that the paschal lamb should be taken up (Ex. 12:3), and set apart for that service; on that day therefore Christ our Passover, who was to be sacrificed for us, was publicly showed."[26]

Matthew Henry asserts Jesus was selected on Palm Sunday. He claimed that day was *the* "selection day," the tenth. I am surprised he did not see the illogical

---

[26] Matthew Henry, *Matthew Henry's Commentary on the Whole Bible, Vol. 5*, (McLean, VA: MacDonald Publishing Company), p. 294.

conclusion to what he said: "five days before his death. The Passover was on the fourteenth day of the month...." If Sunday was the tenth—as the day of selection—it would only allow four days, not five, until Passover. But, inconsistency seems to pervade in explaining the events of the Passion week. A contemporary scholar, Ray Vander Laan, in his book, *Echoes of His Presence*, also agrees with the interpretation Jesus was selected when he rode into Jerusalem.[27] Now, of course, not everyone selected him as the Messiah, but then, not everyone in Egypt (or later in Israel) prepared a lamb. The unbelievers in both cases rejected what God was doing.

The policies state the lamb was selected on the tenth and slain on the fourteenth. If Sunday was the tenth, the crucifixion would be on *Thursday*, the fourteenth, not Friday! This pattern more accurately represents and fulfills scripture. I heard a sermon tape (that's right, "tape," it was that long ago) by Chuck Swindoll in which he proposed a Wednesday crucifixion![28] So, I am not alone in thinking Friday is not the best day for Jesus fulfilling scripture. To see how the synoptic gospels and the Gospel of John can be synchronized, see Appendix B.

---

[27] Ray Vander Laan with Judith E. Markham, "Introduction," *Echoes of His Presence: Stories of the Messiah from the People of His Day*, (Colorado Springs: Focus on the Family Publishing, 1996), pp. 145 and 147.

[28] I loaned the tape and never got it back. Therefore, I cannot give the sermon date.

Simply put, this scenario better fits the scriptures than the historically taught understanding. First, *a Sunday selection and a Thursday slaying more accurately depict the prophetic picture of the Passover lamb.* Second, *it better fulfills Christ's self-prophecy* found in Matthew chapter 12, "For as Jonah was three days and three nights in the belly of a huge fish, so the Son of Man will be three days and three nights in the heart of the earth" (Matt. 12:40). Either Jesus meant what he said or he didn't. If he did mean it, then we should expect him to be in the ground three days and three nights. If he didn't mean it, then how can we trust *anything* he said? Traditional teaching does not allow "three days and three nights" no matter how one contorts the days of the week. With Jesus giving up his spirit at the ninth hour on Friday, it is impossible to conclude "three days and three nights" before a Sunday morning resurrection. We know it was a Sunday resurrection because Matthew 28:1 states, "After the Sabbath, at dawn on the first day of the week, Mary Magdalene and the other Mary went to look at the tomb." The Sabbath was Saturday, and the first day of the week was Sunday.

I realize the first-century inhabitants of Jerusalem may not have been as particular as I am about time. As Ben Witherington III wrote in an article entitled "It's About Time—Easter Time" in the May/June 2016 issue of BAR, "[W]e are a people obsessed with time—and exactness when it comes to time—down to the nanosecond.... They did not obsess about precision when it comes to time."[29] He went on to say:

> In Matthew 12:40 Jesus mentions, "three days *and three nights*," but this is just part of a general analogy with the story of what happened with Jonah and the whale, and as such the time reference shouldn't be pressed. Jesus is just saying, "It will be like the experience of Jonah."[30]

Further he notes: "In fact the phrase 'after three days' in the New Testament can simply mean 'after a while' or 'after a few days' without any clear specificity beyond suggesting several days, in this case parts of three days, would be involved."[31]

Though Witherington may consider my calculations too tedious, I must take issue with his dismissal of biblical literalness. Jesus didn't just say "after three days" but after "three days and three nights." It seems to me he is trying to justify tradition rather than pervade the truth of scripture. Although Witherington has an issue with the timing

---

[29] Ben Witherington III, "It's About Time—Easter Time," *Biblical Archaeology Review*, Vol. 42, No. 3, (Washington, DC: Biblical Archaeology Society, May/June 2016), p. 26.

[30] Ibid.

[31] Ibid.

Jesus put forth as "without any clear specificity," the first-century religious leaders took Jesus' "three days" literally:

> The next day, the one after Preparation Day, the chief priests and the Pharisees went to Pilate. "Sir," they said, "we remember that while he was still alive that deceiver said, 'After three days I will rise again.' So give the order for the tomb to be made secure until the third day. Otherwise, his disciples may come and steal the body and tell the people that he has been raised from the dead. This last deception will be worse than the first."
>
> (MATT. 27:62–64)

With a Thursday crucifixion, Jesus was in the grave before sundown. He was there Thursday night and Friday morning (day 1), Friday night and Saturday morning (day 2), Saturday night and Sunday morning (day 3). Now I realize when the women came to the tomb, it was dark and they could not see; therefore, the above schedule may need to be adjusted to start with the partial day Jesus was in the tomb on Thursday, giving us: Thursday partial day and Thursday evening (day 1), Friday day and evening (day 2), and Saturday day and evening (day3) with Jesus coming out of the tomb before Sunday morning. Use the following figure to work it out yourself.

Jesus the Passover Lamb

Sun 10	Mon 11	Tue 12	Wed 13	Thurs 14	Fri 15	Sat 16	Sun 17
Set Apart Ex. 12:3				Sacrificed Ex. 12:6			
				Day day 1 Eve	Day day 2 Eve	Day day 3 Eve	Morn — Eve

Matthew 12:40

Figure 1

There is one scripture reference not in that figure which needs our consideration—Matthew 28:1. When I heard Chuck Swindoll's sermon in which he placed Christ's passion on Wednesday, this verse was the clincher for me. "After *the Sabbath*, at dawn on the first day of the week, Mary Magdalene and the other Mary went to look at the tomb" (Matt. 28:1, italics mine). What is so interesting about that particular verse? The Greek. In Greek (the language in which the New Testament was written), the word for "Sabbath" is plural! That is right—plural! There had to be *at least two Sabbaths* between the time of the crucifixion and the resurrection! Let. That. Truth. Sink. In.

Combine that thought with the following verse:

Now it was the day of Preparation, and the next day was to be *a special Sabbath*. Because the Jewish leaders did not want the bodies left on the crosses during the Sabbath, they asked Pilate to have the legs broken and the bodies taken down.

(JN. 19:31, ITALICS MINE)

What is a "special Sabbath"? We must first understand the modifier "special." It is the translation of the Greek word *megas* which means "exceedingly, great (-est), high, large, loud, mighty, (be) sore (afraid), strong, to years."[32]

---

[32] Strong, p. 46

In other words it was a great Sabbath—i.e., a Sabbath associated with a feast day.

So, what other connotations did it carry? First, as our Christmas can fall on any day of the week, so could Passover. In 2016, Christmas was on a Sunday. One could say Christmas 2016 was a "special Sunday" or "a great Sunday" or "a high Sunday." If all John was saying is the Passover was to fall on Saturday, then the day of the crucifixion would agree with Christian custom. Second, but John took particular care to make sure his readers understood Jesus died at the same time the Passover lambs were being slaughtered in the Temple area. Since the Passover was treated like a Sabbath (Ex. 12:16), it would be a "special Sabbath." We also see the Sabbath indication in the following passage:

> "The Lord's Passover begins at twilight on the fourteenth day of the first month. On the fifteenth day of that month the Lord's Feast of Unleavened Bread begins; for seven days you must eat bread made without yeast. On the first day *hold a sacred assembly and do no regular work.*"
>
> (Lev. 23:5–7, italics mine)

Therefore, the first day of the Feast of Unleavened Bread was treated as a Sabbath. John could call it "special" because it was not the regular, weekly Sabbath. If Jesus died at the same time as the Passover lambs on Thursday, then the "first day" mentioned in Leviticus 23 where they were to "hold a sacred assembly and do no regular work" would be Friday. Add that together with the regular Sabbath on Saturday and you have a plural number of Sabbaths. Problem solved!

Discipleship Challenge

The Passover is a picture of conversion. Your *personal* Passover is when God comes into your life and calls you to make a decision: *apply the blood or die.*

As can be understood through the exposition of this chapter, Jesus Christ came and fulfilled the shadowy outline and literally became our Passover Lamb! What will you do with the Lamb? What will you do with this Jesus who is the Lamb of God? Will you accept him as your Lord and Savior and apply his blood by faith, or will you ignore his warning? It's an individual choice. What will you choose? Apply the blood or die!

Those of you who have already applied the blood, what are you doing with the Lamb? What are you doing to glorify the Lamb of God? Are you warning others of the coming judgment which promises "death" for the unbeliever? There was a TV commercial shown during January 2003, for a cholesterol lowering drug; at the end, a voice said, "It's your future. Be there." I encourage you if you feel the Holy Spirit tugging at your heart, make your decision to become a follower of Jesus today. *God has a wonderful future for you. Be there.*

I realize much of this chapter flies in the face of practice, custom, and tradition (And history?), as most, if not all, ancient writers believed in a Friday crucifixion. I raise the issue in this chapter as a means to provoke one to think. One should never be dogmatic or use the information posited here to separate oneself from another with a different opinion. Remember, this information is presented to stir conversation, not controversy.

As this chapter closes, the Israelites remained enslaved. *The blood was applied. Life was given. But they were not yet delivered from slavery. What would it take for them to be delivered?* To discover the answer to that question, keep reading.

CHAPTER 3

The Red Sea

An Immersion in Trust

As we saw in the last chapter, the blood of the Passover lamb was shed. The power of Pharaoh was broken. Permission to leave Egypt was granted. But then—*surprise!* Pharaoh changed his mind, *again,* and sent his army after the Israelites to bring them back under his power. As the Israelites took flight, they became boxed in at the Red Sea: the army of Pharaoh was on the west side and the Red Sea was on the east. They needed to cross the Red Sea (Fat chance of that happening!), or they needed to reverse course and fight. What was one to do? God provided a way through the Red Sea and brought them all to safety. As will become evident as we progress, *crossing the*

Red Sea was a shadow of Christian baptism. Though it was just summarized for you, you may want to pause and read Exodus chapter 14 in its entirety.

The meaning of this chapter was the easiest to comprehend. The interpretation of this type is given to us in the New Testament:

> For I do not want you to be ignorant of the fact, brothers and sisters, that our ancestors were all under the cloud and that they all passed through the sea. They were all baptized into Moses in the cloud and in the sea.
>
> (1 COR. 10:1–2)

Almost all will agree the nation of Israel passing through the Red Sea is a type of which the antitype is Christian baptism. The apostle Paul made that connection for us; it is not guess work on our part. As we investigate this event, we will find several *dynamic* things happened at the Red Sea which also happen at Christian baptism.

A New Way of Life

The *first* thing one will notice which also has its parallel in the New Testament is at the Red Sea, *the Israelites were cut off from their previous way of life.* Upon word from

Pharaoh that they were permitted to leave, the Israelites departed Egypt immediately. They did not delay to see if the Pharaoh would treat them better. The situation in Egypt had to be separated from the new life they were to live. The same is true for us. We must cut off the influence of the sin nature when we pass through the waters of baptism. Sometimes this means the negative influence of family, friends, and coworkers—we overlook such influences to our own peril. When we repent of the life we have lived, we must leave it, or we may be tempted to return to it.

This may be one of the reasons God led the nation to the edge of the sea: He directed them to the place where they would have to make a decision. They could go back to Pharaoh and possibly die, or they could follow Moses and go through the Red Sea—literally cutting themselves off from their previous way of life. That same decision is put into the lap of every new disciple of Christ: go back and serve the devil and the flesh, or follow Jesus through the waters of baptism and start a new life. Please note, as Moses preceded the Israelites through the Red Sea, so also Jesus preceded New Testament believers in water baptism by submitting to the baptism of John the Baptist "to fulfill all righteousness."[33]

---

[33] Matt. 3:15

Christian baptism is for the penitent[34] only. It is for believers only; without faith, one only gets wet. The writer of Hebrews puts it this way:

> By faith he kept the Passover and the sprinkling of blood, so that the destroyer of the firstborn would not touch the firstborn of Israel. By faith the people passed through the Red Sea as on dry land; but when the Egyptians tried to do so, they were drowned.
>
> (HEB. 11:28–29)

"By faith…kept the Passover; by faith…passed through the Sea." Following the commands of Moses took faith. Following the commands of Jesus takes faith. This is not something someone else chooses for you; it is something you must choose for yourself.

This is the shadowy outline the Israelites left for the Christian. The Israelites had faith in YHWH and his prophet, Moses. By faith they slew a lamb on the fourteenth and applied its blood to the doorposts of their houses. Then, also by faith, they came to the point of decision to follow Moses through the waters of the Red Sea or stay where they were. The blood had been applied but

---

[34] Acts 2:38

they would still be in Egypt, in bondage, if they did not go through.

Note: When the Israelites went through the sea (were baptized), they had already had the blood applied. I only mention this because there is some sharp disagreement within Christendom about when the blood of Jesus is applied to the believer's life. By the order of the types, we must conclude it is before—not during or after—baptism.

Today, the person comes to Christ. By faith, the blood is applied. Now, one comes to the point of decision: Will he or she take the next step of faith and publicly confess his or her faith through baptism? I am surprised by the number of "blood applied" confessors who have not taken this step of obedience. Why?

Passing through the Red Sea was not an option for the Israelites; they would have either died or been conscripted into Pharaoh's service once again, even though they had had the blood of the lamb applied. Had Moses told the people to go through the Red Sea, but it was not neces-sary for them to be free, how many do you suppose would have ventured into the sea "with a wall of water on their right and on their left"?[35] Or if Moses had said to them it was only a symbolic gesture, how many would have will-ingly gone through for something unneeded and only

---

[35] Ex. 14:22

figurative? Some of you have probably had similar advice from well-meaning Christians. (See excursus below.)

The Israelites' previous life was behind them. They had to go forward if they wanted to be free. Christian baptism has the same expectation. If you want to be free of the sin and shame that have plagued your life to this point, you must—by faith—go forward. You must pass through the waters of baptism. No other logical or scriptural alternative presents itself—in shadow or substance. Notice again how final the Israelites' decision was. Once the sea closed there was no easy way back! Their decision was sealed as tightly as the returning waters sealed the seam they had just walked through.

Sarah Jo Sarchet is a (Presbyterian) pastor in Chicago. One time, a 10 year-old boy in her congregation named Cameron, walked into her office and said he needed to talk to her. Fresh from soccer practice, and wearing his Cincinnati Reds baseball cap, he had a request for her. "I'd like to be baptized," he said. "We were learning about Jesus' baptism in Sunday School. The teacher asked the class who was baptized, and all the other kids raised their hands. I want to be baptized too."

Using her best pastoral care tone of voice, she said, "Cameron, do you really want to be baptized because everyone else is?" His freckles winked up at her and he replied, "No. I want to be baptized because it means I belong to God."

She was touched by his understanding. "Well, then," she said. "How about this Sunday?" His smile turned to concern and he asked, "Do I have to be baptized in front of all those people in the church? Can't I just have a friend baptize me in the river?" She asked where he came up with that idea. "Well, Jesus was baptized by his cousin John in a river, wasn't he?"

Caught off guard, she conceded, "You have a point. But, if a friend baptized you in the river, how would the church know about it?" Realizing this was a teachable moment, she climbed up on her foot stool to reach for a book that was located on the highest shelf. But before she placed her hand on the book, he responded.

"I guess by my new way of living," he said.

She nearly fell off the foot stool and left the book on the shelf. Cameron's understanding was neither child-ish nor simple. It was profound. Baptism calls us to a new way of living.[36]

One can claim the blood has been applied, and even publicly be baptized. But the truth of one's salvation will

---

[36] "From a sermon by Sarah Jo Sarchet preached at Fourth Presbyterian Church in Chicago," January 9, 2015, Northfield United Methodist Parish Page, accessed July 18, 2017, https://www.facebook.com/permalink. php?id=153069421385186&story_fbid=1054872024538250.

be seen by the change in his or her life, their *new* life, their *born again* life. The following will demonstrate that more happened at the Red Sea than just establishing a new way of life.

A Declaration of Allegiance to God

The *second* thing one should notice in passing through the sea is *each one declared his allegiance to God*. At the seaside, the Israelites had to decide who would be their Lord. Would they return to Egypt and serve Pharaoh, or go forward and serve the God that redeemed them from slavery? In other words, they had to declare their allegiance!

I submit to you, those who will not take a step *forward* are in danger of taking a huge step *backward*. I have heard some compare the Christian life to a conveyor belt. One is either moving forward or is sliding backward. Standing still is the same as losing ground. Moving forward is a sign of faith and obedience. The people of faith need to pursue the will of another—the will of Father God. The old way of life was determined by oneself (or a taskmaster), but the new way of life is to be determined by the Lord. How can he be your Lord if you do not do what he says? As Jesus once said, "Why do you call me, 'Lord, Lord,' and do not do what I say?" (Lk. 6:46). So the question is, "In what way did the Israelites show allegiance to God?"

> As Pharaoh approached, the Israelites looked up, and there were the Egyptians, marching after them. They were terrified and cried out to the Lord. They said to Moses, "Was it because there were no graves in Egypt that you brought us to the desert to die? What have you done to us by bringing us out of Egypt? Didn't we say to you in Egypt, 'Leave us alone; let us serve the Egyptians'? It would have been better for us to serve the Egyptians than to die in the desert!"
>
> (Ex. 14:10–12)

They *cried to the Lord* and complained to Moses. That isn't perfect faith; it is childish faith. But at least, it is faith! Didn't Jesus say something somewhere about coming to him as a little child?[37] In their distress, they cried out to YHWH, not another god. That took faith, especially after growing up under the influence of the idols and temples of Egypt. Moses and YHWH got them into this mess; now they wanted YHWH and Moses to get them out of it. So God did the impossible! When I first preached these messages, there was an NFL commercial airing where a man

---

[37] Mk. 10:15

was talking about the word "impossible." He declared (and showed clips of) all the amazing comebacks and acrobatic moves people thought could not be done. He then closed with the statement the players "have made the impossible, possible." It is impossible to part water, but God made the impossible, possible. You see, God *majors* in the impossible. Here is the way the psalmist Asaph would later recount this event:

> "With your mighty arm you redeemed your people,
>   the descendants of Jacob and Joseph.
> The waters saw you, God,
>   the waters saw you and writhed;
>   the very depths were convulsed.
> The clouds poured down water,
>   the heavens resounded with thunder;
>   your arrows flashed back and forth.
> Your thunder was heard in the whirlwind,
>   your lightning lit up the world;
>   the earth trembled and quaked.
> Your path led through the sea,
>   your way through the mighty waters,
>   though your footprints were not seen.
> You led your people like a flock
>   by the hand of Moses and Aaron."
>
> (Ps. 77:15–20)

Again, we read Hebrews 11:29, "By faith the people passed through the Red Sea as on dry land; but when the Egyptians tried to do so, they were drowned." This tells us the Israelites went through by faith but their enemies were destroyed by a lack of faith. The Israelites were looking at God as their redeemer, their deliverer; the Egyptians were looking at man—i.e., the Israelites—*If they can do it, so can we.*

What does that mean for us? Never go through the waters of baptism looking at another person (best friend, pastor, etc.). You are to be swearing your allegiance to God, not your friend, not your pastor, not even to your church! When we recognize the great work God has done to bring us salvation, we should give our allegiance to him and his deliverer, Jesus Christ of whom Moses was simply a shadow. The initial way to declare one's allegiance is through faith, confession, repentance, and baptism.

A Declaration of Allegiance to God's Appointed Leader

Not only did the Red Sea experience challenge the Israelites to swear allegiance to God, but also to his appointed leader, Moses. Exodus 14 states it this way:

And when the Israelites saw the mighty hand of the Lord displayed against the Egyptians, the people feared the Lord and put their trust in him *and in Moses his servant.*

(Ex. 14:31, ITALICS MINE)

Most Americans I know struggle with following another human being—with giving allegiance to another imperfect person. I understand. Humans are fallible; they make mistakes. I have never met a perfect person and certainly not a perfect elder or pastor. They don't exist. Therefore, since they are not perfect, we struggle to follow their lead—even though God has appointed them to their respective positions. Moses was not perfect. And yet, despite this fact, God expected the people to listen to him and obey his words as the very words of God.

The Lord said to Moses, "I am going to come to you in a dense cloud, so that the people will hear me speaking with you and will always put their trust in you." Then Moses told the Lord what the people had said.

(Ex. 19:9)

God expects us to follow our appointed leaders, just as they follow Christ[38] of course. To be a faithful Christian,

---

[38] 1 Cor. 11:1

one must learn to be submissive and obedient to the local church leadership.

> Have confidence in your leaders and submit to their authority, because they keep watch over you as those who must give an account. Do this so that their work will be a joy, not a burden, for that would be of no advantage to you.
>
> (HEB. 13:17)

As part of a democratic society, we believe we have rights. That is true as an American, but is this country your first allegiance? Isn't your first allegiance now to Christ? Your rights were abolished when you chose to follow God and whatever leader he chooses to appoint. Submit to the authority of God's chosen leaders(s).

One Receives a New Identity

As the waters of the Red Sea came back together, the people received a new identity. They were now *God's redeemed*, baptized into Moses; they were *no longer slaves*. In one action—passing through a body of water—they went from being Pharaoh's to being God's, from being slaves to being a free nation.

After we pass through the waters of Christian baptism

we receive a new identity. We are now Christ's redeemed, no longer slaves to sin. We have a new master by whose name we are called—*Christ*ian. An important transaction happens there; one goes from lost to saved, from pagan to Christian, from sinner to saint.

I remember attending my thirty-fifth high school class reunion. One of the ladies there discovered I was a preacher. She started going around from table to table saying, "Did you know Bill Thomas is a preacher?" (You would have thought Hitler had been converted!) I had a new identity. It could not be denied. It could not be kept hidden. When a person becomes a Christian, one commits oneself to Jesus Christ and…

One Commits to a New Direction

They needed to learn a new way of living under their new leader, Moses. God took them to Mt. Sinai and gave them rules so their new lives could be governed by the Law and by Moses. No longer would they huddle around the mud pits of Egypt; they were headed in a new direction. They were going to the Promised Land!

We have also received the word of God, the Bible, and are to apply it as led—not by Moses, but by the Spirit of Jesus, the Holy Spirit. We are to no longer huddle around the mud pits of sin. We have new lives, are committed to a new way of life, and are headed for a new heaven and new earth. "But in keeping with his promise we are looking forward *to a new heaven and a new earth*, where righteousness dwells" (2 Pet. 3:13, italics mine). We will investigate the Promised Land in our final chapter after we look at the wilderness journey and passing through the Jordan River at flood stage. Before we move on from the Red Sea experience, though, I would like you to consider this. Allow me the liberty of this fictitious tale:

There are always stragglers, aren't there? Well, the day the Israelites crossed the Red Sea on dry ground was probably no exception. Abdiel and Yassai were taking their time as they walked and talked.

Yassai: I don't know about you, but I am getting fed up with Moses calling all the shots.

Abdiel: I understand how you feel, but he has gotten Pharaoh to release us; and now we are going in a new direction—to the Promised Land!

Yassai: Yeh, but things were not really that bad for me. I had a nice mudbrick home and worked the fields for grain.

Abdiel: That's okay for you, but I was the one stomping the straw into the mud to make those bricks! I can tell you, it was hard labor!

Yassai: I'm sorry, but I had a comfortable living

and really don't like picking up everything and moving. Maybe Pharaoh is a changed man. Maybe those ten plagues—the last one even affecting his son—has mellowed him, and he will treat us better. He must be humble now, having seen the power of YHWH displayed for us, his people. I'm thinking about going back. Do you want to come with me?

Abdiel: Are you crazy? Don't you know what awaits you? Do you think those soldiers back there are here to give us safe passage back? I am glad we are out of there! I am going with Moses, and I am going to the Promised Land!

Yassai: Suit yourself. I'm going back and serving Pharaoh.

Yassai turned and started back. "Goodbye, my friend. Good luck with that Moses fellow." He continued to walk back toward Egypt. In the distance, he could see the soldiers just beginning to enter the path through the sea. "They'll be glad to see me," he thought. He continued to walk toward the soldiers and the soldiers continued to drive their chariots toward him. As they neared one another, Yassai cried out, "Hey! I'm back, fellas." The last thing Yassai experienced was the tip of an Egyptian spear piercing his belly.[39]

---

[39] Author's original.

The purpose of that fictitious story is to alert the reader to the mixed feelings the Israelites emoted as they crossed the Red Sea. It is important to realize the mixed crowd Moses led through the sea, because their diverse views would come to the forefront as he continued to lead them through the wilderness.

They were beginning a new way of life free from slavery. They had sworn allegiance to YHWH and to his appointed leader, Moses. They had taken on a new identity and were headed in a new direction. But, they were taking Egypt with them in their hearts. The best sermon series I have ever heard on this topic was preached by my former mentor, Bishop Joey Johnson of The House of the Lord in Akron, Ohio. The series was entitled "The Ravages of Rejection." If you call their church office you might be able to secure a copy of the series.

Excurses

In this chapter the crossing of the Red Sea has been compared to Christian baptism. What does the New Testament say about water baptism? A number of scriptures will be examined to see if we can come to a consensus. Like the previous chapter, it will be best serve the reader to temporarily forfeit one's preconceived notions and traditions.

This topic will be examined under three headings: mode, purpose, and recipients.

Mode

Once upon a time there was a young boy with a mother, father, and older brother. One day, the young boy came into the house from playing in the yard with some friends. He was filthy! His mother took one look at him and said, "Go upstairs and take a bath immediately. Dinner is almost ready."

On his way up the stairs, he met his brother who was coming down the stairs. "What are you doing?" he inquired.

"Mom told me I had to take a bath."

"Oh, you don't need to take a bath. Just wash your hands and face and come back down."

Being older and wiser, the younger brother believed his brother knew what he was talking about, even though it seemed clear to him it wasn't what his mother wanted. He washed his hands and face and took his place at the dining table.

When his mother came to the table, do you think she was pleased with the younger son's appearance? Do you think the younger son was obedient to what he had been told by his mother? Most readers would respond with a resounding "No!" to each question.[40]

Throughout the history of the church, many denominations have chosen to apply a small amount of water (henceforth referred to as "sprinkle") to the head of the baptismal candidate. Others pour water over the head of the one being baptized. Still others perform immersion of the whole body of the baptismal candidate. This is the question of mode—how should baptism be performed? One must wonder (at least, I do) why there are so many variations.

If we return to our story for a moment, the mother in the story is the Mother Church proclaiming the good news of Jesus. The younger son is one who is coming to Christ, and the older son represents the clergy. The confusion over mode seems to have started with the last one. For whatever reasons, many clergy decided to perform baptisms by a mode other than what was originally given in scripture.

What was originally given in scripture? Our word "baptism" is not a translation of the Greek language, but rather, it is a transliteration (a letter for letter conversion to the English language). The Greek word is *baptisma*—i.e., baptism. According to W.E. Vine it means "…consisting of

---

[40] Author's original.

the processes of immersion, submersion and emergence (from *bapto*, 'to dip'), is used (a) of John's 'baptism,' (b) of Christian 'baptism.'"[41]

The New International Dictionary of New Testament Theology Volume 1 defines baptism as:

In secular Greek *bapto* means (a) dip, (b) dip into dye, and so dye, and (c) draw (water). *Baptizo* is an intensive form of *bapto* and means (a) dip, and (b) cause to perish (as by drowning a man or a sinking ship).

While there is some evidence that *bapto* was occasionally used in secular Greek of a ritual bath, there is none to show that *baptizo* was so employed (perhaps because of its association with the idea of perishing)....

Despite assertions to the contrary, it seems that *baptizo*, both in Jewish and Christian contexts, normally meant "immerse," and that even when it became a technical term for baptism, the thought of immersion remains.[42]

~G. R. Beasley-Murray

These dictionary definitions concur—the biblical mode of baptism is immersion. Beasley-Murray records

---

[41] W.E. Vine, *An Expository Dictionary of New Testament Words*, (Old Tappan, NJ: Fleming H. Revell Company, 1966), pp. 96–97.

[42] Colin Brown, *The New International Dictionary of New Testament Theology, Vol. 1*, (Grand Rapids, MI: Zondervan, 1975), p.144.

an interesting, but little known, aspect in his article—*baptizo* was connected to drowning or perishing. That reminds one of Romans 6:3, "Or don't you know that all of us who were baptized into Christ Jesus were baptized into his *death*?" (italics mine). Having looked at the meaning of the Greek word, it seems best to understand the biblical—and therefore, most obedient—mode of baptism is by immersion.

I grew up sporadically attending the Presbyterian Church. I had never seen an immersion. But once I understood the biblical meaning of the word—even though it went against my previous training—I was eager to be immersed. Next, we need to examine the purpose of baptism.

Purpose

As was seen in our investigation of mode, there is also a difference of opinion about *why* someone is baptized. Baptism did not originate with either Jesus or John the Baptist. Baptism—in the form of self-immersion—was already a well-known act in Israel. Evidence is found in the Qumran community around the Dead Sea, which most commentators believe to be Essenes. In the *Community Rule* (1QS) we find the application of water is more than symbolic but is considered important for purification:

He shall not be justified by that which his stubborn heart declares lawful, for seeking the ways of light he looks toward darkness. He shall not be reckoned among the perfect; he shall neither be purified by atonement, nor cleansed by purifying waters, nor sanctified by seas and rivers, nor washed clean with any ablution.[43] (1QS, column V)

The one who was stubborn in heart would not be purified no matter what type of water application was made. The heart needed to be made right before he self-immersed (the practice of the Qumran community). Further, pious Jews of the first century were also practicing self-immersion. Excavations have discovered *miqva'ot*[44] at Qumran and in various places throughout Jerusalem. Many in the Christian faith believe the sole purpose of water baptism is to identify with Jesus Christ in his death, burial, and resurrection. Identify—nothing more, nothing less. One example is radio Bible teacher Chuck Swindoll who has written, "While it isn't essential for salvation, it is cer-

---

[43] Geza Vermes, *The Complete Dead Sea Scrolls in English*, (New York: Penguin Press, 1997), p. 100.

[44] *Miqva'ot* is the plural of *miqveh*, a Jewish ritual immersion bath for the purpose of removing ritual impurity (see Mark 7:4, "wash"). An excellent article on *miqva'ot* can be found in *Biblical Archaeology Review*, Jan/Feb. 1987, "Discovering What Jewish Miqva'ot Can Tell Us About Christian Baptism."

tainly expected of the believer."[45] Another example comes from the prolific pen of Francis Chan:

> "When first-century Christians took this step of *identifying* themselves with the death and resurrection of Jesus, they were publicly declaring their allegiance to Christ. This immediately marked them for martyrdom—all of the hostility that the world felt toward Jesus would now be directed at them. Baptism was a declaration that a person's life, identity, and priorities were centered on Jesus and His mission. Depending on where you live in the world, you may not see the same reaction to your choice to be baptized, but that act of *identifying with Christ* is essential, no matter where you live."[46] (italics mine)

I deeply respect the ministries of these two men, but I find myself at odds with them concerning the purpose of baptism. When approaching the subject of baptism, I find many want to argue their denomination's position rather than simply taking the Bible at its word.

The attention of the New Testament believer needs

---

[45] Charles R. Swindoll, *Growing Deep in the Christian Life*, (Portland: Multnomah Press, 1986), p. 365.

[46] Francis Chan with Mark Beuving, *Multiply: Disciples Making Disciples*, (Colorado Springs: David C Cook, 2012), p. 32.

to focus on what the New Testament scriptures say. Acts 2:38 seems a good place to start:

> Peter replied, "Repent and be baptized, every one of you, in the name of Jesus Christ *for the forgiveness of your sins.* And you will receive the gift of the Holy Spirit." (italics mine)

On the Day of Pentecost, the twelve apostles[47] were filled with the Holy Spirit, spoke in tongues, and a great crowd gathered to see what the commotion was about. Peter stood up, along with the other Apostles and addressed the crowd. He preached convincingly that Jesus is the Messiah (Gr., Christ), and the crowd's leaders had killed the Messiah. In a panic (and under conviction), the people asked what they were to do. Verse 38, above, was Peter's response. In it Peter gave them the cure for their dilemma which included the purpose for baptism: "for the forgiveness of sins."

The late Donald Nash, Greek professor at Kentucky Christian College (now University), wrote extensively about this in his book, *Problem Passages Probed*:

> Some are adopting an old dogma that the preposition "for" (*eis* in the Greek) in Acts 2:38 should be translated "because of" instead of "in order to."

---

[47] See fuller explanation in Chapter 5.

The linguistic meaning of *eis* seems to be obvious from the context of Acts 2:38. The people at Pentecost had asked what to do, evidently meaning to rid themselves of sin's guilt. Peter told them to do two things: "repent" and "be baptized." If they were already in the state of forgiveness and already had the Holy Spirit he would have just said, "Do nothing, you are o.k."

It is interesting to note that this phrase "for the remission of sin" in Acts 2:38 is the very same phrase (*eis aphesin hamartion*) as in Matthew 26:28. Jesus said His blood was to be shed for the remission of sin. Therefore, if baptism in Acts 2:38 is "because your sins have already been forgiven" then Jesus was dying "because sins had already been forgiven," which is manifest absurdity.[48]

His writing continued as he quoted a number of Greek specialists with the same opinion. He mentioned Henry B. Dewing, Henry Darling Brackett, Frank Hugh Foster, Edgar Goodspeed, and *Kittel's Theological Dictionary of the New Testament*.[49]

If the blood was applied before the baptism (referring to the shadow in the Old Testament—see previous chapter),

---

[48] Donald A. Nash, *Problem Passages Probed*, (Grayson, KY: Witness Press, 1985), p. 120.

[49] Nash, pp. 121–122

then how can Acts 2:38 be true? I know two things: (1) scripture does not contradict scripture; (2) the scriptures clearly teach baptism is a *part* of one's salvation. (How big a part, only God knows.) "Whoever believes and is baptized will be *saved*, but whoever does not believe will be condemned" (Mk. 16:16, marginal reading, italics mine).

> For Christ also suffered once for sins, the righteous for the unrighteous, to bring you to God. He was put to death in the body but made alive in the Spirit. After being made alive, he went and made proclamation to the imprisoned spirits—to those who disobeyed long ago when God waited patiently in the days of Noah while the ark was being built. In it only a few people, eight in all, were *saved* through water, and this water symbolizes *baptism that now saves you also*—not the removal of dirt from the body but the pledge of a clear conscience toward God. *It saves you by the resurrection of Jesus Christ*, who has gone into heaven and is at God's right hand—with angels, authorities and powers in submission to him.
>
> (1 PET. 3:18–22, ITALICS MINE)

"Baptism that now saves you also…. It saves you by the resurrection of Jesus Christ." It seems clear from those two phrases, baptism has a salvific nature. In neither of those passages is the blood mentioned, but curiously, the resurrection is mentioned in the latter. Why would Peter mention the resurrection in association with baptism? Interestingly, the apostle Paul mentions the resurrection as a link to salvation as well.

> But if it is preached that Christ has been raised from the dead, how can some of you say that there is no resurrection of the dead? *If there is no resurrection of the dead, then not even Christ has been raised. And if Christ has not been raised, our preaching is useless and so is your faith.* More than that, we are then found to be false witnesses about God that he raised Christ from the dead. But he did not raise him if in fact the dead are not raised. For if the dead are not raised, then Christ has not been raised either. *And if Christ has not been raised, your faith is futile; you are still in your sins.* Then those also who have fallen asleep in Christ are lost. If only for this life we have hope in Christ, we are of all people most to be pitied.
>
> (1 COR. 15:12–19, ITALICS MINE)

Without the resurrection, our faith is "useless" and "futile" and we are "still in [our] sins." The resurrection verified everything Jesus proclaimed. If he had not been raised, then he would have been just another self-deluded, self-appointed, false messiah. But he has been raised! And therefore, his resurrection is connected to our salvation. Peter linked his resurrection to baptism (1 Pet. 3:21), and Paul connected Jesus' resurrection to salvation in 1 Corinthians 15:12–19 and in Romans 10:9–10.

> If you declare with your mouth, "Jesus is Lord," and believe in your heart that God *raised him from the dead, you will be saved.* For it is with your heart that you believe and are justified, and it is with your mouth that you profess and *are saved.*
>
> (ROM. 10:9–10, ITALICS MINE).

The conclusion of the matter, it seems, is we are baptized for the [purpose of] forgiveness of sins (Acts 2:38) and that happens by association with his resurrection (1 Pet. 3:21).

Either/or and both/and thinking

Some will read this excursus and dismiss it because it makes much of 1 Peter 3:21. Others will charge, "Hey, Bill, what about salvation by grace through faith as in Ephesians 2:8?" I believe that verse. The problem is, too often in Biblical interpretation, we have an either/or mentality when it is not called for. In other words, either passage A carries the weight of evidence or passage B

carries the weight of evidence. That seems to be a danger-
ous way of thinking in many cases, salvation being one.
If students of the word follow that philosophy to the end,
they will find themselves questioning whether they are
saved by Jesus or by the Father. Isn't it both? When more
than one passage discusses how one is to be saved, what
gives us the audacity to pick one passage over another?
Can't they both (or all) be true…be truth?

When I was in my first pastorate, a lady came to my
office for a chat (I can't remember who initiated the visit).
As we talked, it became clear that she was practicing baptism "in the name of Jesus" only (Acts 2:38, 10:48). She
was even re-baptizing those who had previously been
baptized "in the name of the Father, the Son, and the Holy
Spirit" (Matt. 28:19). I asked her—if both phrases were
used in the New Testament, why she believed only one
formula was correct. She obviously had either/or thinking.
She mentioned "the name" in Matthew 28 is Jesus—Jesus
is the name of the Father, the Son, and the Holy Spirit
(so she believes is the proper understanding of Ephesians
3:14–15). She was presenting a modern form of modalism. Modalism was condemned as heretical as early as the
second century AD[50] I would have had no problem with

---

[50] "What are the beliefs of Jesus only/oneness Pentecostals?" GotQuestions.
org, accessed August 1, 2017, https://www.gotquestions.org/oneness-
Jesus-only.html.

her "in the name of Jesus" baptism if she wasn't so dogmatic it was the only correct way. I thought either way would suffice. She was either/or; I was both/and. I ended the conversation by suggesting she worship elsewhere. I did not want her influence in the congregation.

Since all scripture is inspired by the Holy Spirit, shouldn't we take a both/and attitude at many junctures? Rather than saying we are saved by either 1 Peter 3:21 or by Ephesians 2:8, or either by Romans 10:9–10 or Acts 2:38, why not include them all? So…are we saved by our confession…or by baptism…or faith? Yes. Yes. Yes. When there is more than one scripture informing one how to be saved, why do we have to choose just one way instead of including them all? Why do we too often only consider either/or instead of both/and scenarios?

Mode—immersion; purpose—the remission of sins; recipients…

The Recipients

Who should be baptized? Infants? Children? Adolescents? Adults? Believers? Unbelievers? What about baptism by proxy? Do we want the biblical answers or the answers of our faith tradition? I only ask that because some people have never taken the time to search this out for themselves. What do the scriptures say? Many have simply accepted what their "older brother" has told them. I challenge you to pick up an exhaustive concordance of the Bible and do a study for yourself. Forget what I have written. Forget what your denomination has taught you. Look at the scriptures for scripture's sake. Look up every reference to "baptism" and every reference to "save" and then make up your own mind.

The conclusion I have come to—having done what I just challenged you to do—is baptism is for those of sufficient age to:

- understand the meaning of sin,
- have the ability and desire to repent of their sin,
- have developed a faith in Jesus, and
- confess him as Lord and Savior.

As Beasley-Murray wrote in his article on baptism, and with which I concur:

The present writer believes that infant baptism is excluded from the horizon of the apostolic writers, not alone by its apparent lack of mention in their writings, but by their equation of the gift of baptism with the gift of faith.[51]

---

[51] Brown, p. 149

Is Baptism a Work?

One objection still remains. There are those who will claim baptism is a "work" because the person must "do" something. *Everyone*, no matter what their theology, believes the one coming to Christ must "do" something to be saved! Some say we must confess Christ (Rom. 10:9–10)—confession is *doing* something. Some say we must be baptized (the majority of this chapter)—baptism is *doing* something. Others say one must only believe—believing is *doing* something. If one wants to discuss works, look at Jesus' own words about belief: "Jesus answered, 'The *work* of God is this: *to believe* in the one he has sent'" (Jn. 6:29, italics mine). Technically then, *belief is a work*! The person coming to Christ must believe—that is *doing* something. Those who wish to claim baptism is a work and we are saved apart from works (Eph. 2:8–10) should remember the recipient of baptism is in the passive, not active, role—he or she is *being* baptized. Someone else is doing the action, *the work*. If baptism is a work, it is a work of God. He is the one working on the now believer's heart. He is the one cleansing the sinner of his or her sins.

One of the reasons baptism has become a divisive issue in the church is because many in the church have not followed the biblical example set forth for us. The biblical example is to baptize the believers the same day they come to faith and make their confessions of faith (Acts 2:38–41; 8:34–38; 9:17–19; 10:44–48; 16:13–15; 16:31–34; 19:4–5).

One may wonder how I interact with those who disagree with what has been expressed in this chapter. I treat them the same way I treat all who disagree with me on any point of doctrine. I love them. But more than that, if a person claims to be a born-again follower of Jesus Christ—even though they may have experienced a different mode of baptism or participated for a different reason than I did—I treat them as a brother or sister in Christ. If they claim to be in the family, I treat them like family.

Discipleship Challenge

There are actually two challenges for this chapter. First, are you willing to set aside your denomination's teachings and traditions and study the scriptures alone and draw your own conclusions? Following my earlier challenge of using an exhaustive concordance to look up "baptize[d]/ baptism" and "save/saved/salvation" is a good start.

Second, if you have never been water baptized, why not? As Ananias said to Saul, "And now what are you waiting for? Get up, be baptized and wash your sins away, calling on his name" (Acts 22:16). If you have never been baptized, *do so quickly for the glory of God.*

PART TWO

THE JOURNEY IN THE WILDERNESS

CHAPTER 4

THE WILDERNESS JOURNEY

A Time of Testing

B efore we move further into the story of the Israelites, time to review is in order. In Chapter 1, the shadows of Egypt, Pharaoh, and Moses were interpreted as the sin nature, Satan, and Jesus Christ, respectively. Chapter 2 challenged us with understanding the Passover in relation to Jesus Christ as our Passover Lamb who brings us redemption. That chapter also suggested a literal understanding of the Passover as fulfilled in the death of Jesus needed a change in the traditional time sequence. Chapter 3 viewed the Israelites as they passed through the waters of the Red Sea and understood that as a type of

Christian baptism. The current chapter delves into their story as they journeyed beyond the Red Sea and through the wilderness.

President George W. Bush, in an airport lobby, noticed a man in a long flowing white robe with a long flowing white beard and flowing white hair. The man had a staff in one hand and some stone tablets under the other arm. President George W Bush approached the man and inquired, "Aren't you Moses." The man ignored President George W. Bush and stared at the ceiling.

President George W. Bush positioned himself more directly in the man's view and asked again, "Aren't you Moses?" The man continued to peruse the ceiling.

President George W. Bush tugged at the man's sleeve and asked once again, "Aren't you Moses?"

The man finally responded in an irritated voice, "Yes, I am."

President George W. Bush asked him why he was so irritated and the man replied, "The last time a bush spoke to me, I ended up spending forty years in the wilderness."[52]

---

[52] "President George W Bush and Moses Joke," Free Funny Jokes, accessed July 19, 2017, http://www.free-funny-jokes.com/george-and-moses.html.

The scope of this chapter is to investigate the period of time from the crossing of the Red Sea until the crossing of the Jordan River. This is the time they journeyed in the wilderness for forty years. That's right—the man said forty years! Though Numbers 32:13 says they "wandered," I prefer the word "journeyed." *Wandered* has the connotation of doing something with no purpose or end in sight—which is how many of them probably felt. *Journeyed* resonates with purpose. Since they had the leading of the cloud by day and pillar of fire by night, it seems they were on a journey—directed and purposeful—if for no other reason than to await the last unfaithful Israelite to die. We will get to that in a moment.

Instead of examining every detail of their journey, I have chosen to highlight key events that manifested the hearts of the people. The forty-year wilderness journey is a shadow of *the carnal or worldly Christian*. Isn't that an oxymoron? One would think so, but that is what the apostle Paul stated the Corinthian believers to be. "Brothers and sisters, I could not address you as people who live by the Spirit but as people who are still worldly—mere infants in Christ. I gave you milk, not solid food, for you were not yet ready for it. Indeed, you are still not ready" (1 Cor. 3:1–2). The word translated "worldly" is the Greek word *sarkino* which comes from the word *sarx*, flesh.[53]

---

[53] Strong, p. 64

Therefore, they were "worldly" (NIV) or acting out of the flesh, "carnal" (KJV, NKJV).

The Israelites were very excited after they passed through the Red Sea and the Egyptians were drowned. I wonder: *How long did it take for the thrill of victory at the Red Sea to dissipate?* A week? A month? A year? How about three days?!

> Then Moses led Israel from the Red Sea and they went into the Desert of Shur. For *three days* they traveled in the desert without finding water. When they came to Marah, they could not drink its water because it was bitter. (That is why the place is called Marah.) So the people *grumbled against Moses,* saying, "What are we to drink?"
>
> (EX. 15:22–24, ITALICS MINE)

Grumbling

One of the definitive marks of this period in Israel's history is their persistent grumbling. I want to call them "wandering whiners" but feel that is too derogatory—so I won't. What does grumbling designate? It demonstrates they were not really trusting God. Shortly after the water incident at Marah, we read:

In the desert the whole community grumbled against Moses and Aaron. The Israelites said to them, "If only we had died by the Lord's hand in Egypt! There we sat around pots of meat and ate all the food we wanted, but you have brought us out into this desert to starve this entire assembly to death."

(Ex. 16:2–3)

Whether they were complaining about circumstances or complaining about Moses and Aaron, they were really complaining about God. When one grumbles or complains, he or she is saying that God is not acting justly toward them—God is not giving them what they need (translated, "want"). *Not enough water. We don't like the food. We don't like the leadership.* They were barely out of Egypt and *already,* they were wanting "the good old days."

Isn't it odd how time, distance, and a lack of comfort can make one forget? Oh, they had plenty of water back in Egypt, but *they were slaves!* The pots of meat were plentiful, but *they were slaves!* They didn't have Moses and Aaron calling the shots, but *they were slaves*—they never got to call the shots! How could they forget so quickly? Discomfort. What does the New Testament say? "Do all things without grumbling or disputing; so that you will prove yourselves to be blameless and innocent, children of God..." (Phil. 2:14–15, NASB).

Are you ever like the Israelites? *This crummy old car! This run-down pile of sticks I live in!* When the car breaks down or the furnace blows cold air in the winter, we are discomfited. When we are discomfited, we feel we have the *right* to grumble and complain! We don't care what the problem is: water, food, shelter, leadership—we grumble. The following principle does not set well with us independent thinking Americans: When one rejects God's chosen leaders, he or she rejects God's chosen way to lead, and ultimately rejects God's leading. (We covered that in chapter three, didn't we?) Paul also wrote to the Corinthians:

> You are still worldly. For since there is jealousy and quarreling among you, are you not worldly? Are you not acting like mere humans? For when one says, "I follow Paul," and another, "I follow Apollos," are you not mere human beings?
>
> (1 COR. 3:3–4)

When we question our God-given leaders—or even have a strong preference for one over another—we are questioning God. WARNING: Questioning God ultimately leads to disobeying God. When we begin to question God, we conclude that we know better than he knows. If we know better, then we can do what we think best, even if it is contrary to scripture! "Hey, sweetheart, let's party hardy! After all, we just married off our last child." When we question or grumble against God's leaders and begin to do our own thing, a loss of focus on the things of God is inevitable.

Lost Focus

The Israelites had a second problem. This problem started because God called Moses to the top of the mountain, and he was gone for forty days. Without the visible leadership of Moses, the people lost their focus. One of the attributes of a carnal or worldly Christian is he must have someone to look upon to take on the bulk of the responsibility so he can be free from it. I find it interesting; as much as they rebelled against Moses' leadership, they missed him when he was gone. Being disconnected from the one who was their source of "god-knowledge," they needed a visible sign that God was still with them. Enter the golden calf!

The problem with the golden calf, as with *all* idolatry, is a loss of focus. One focuses on the material instead of the immaterial. One focuses on what can be felt over what can be *faithed*, on the touchable rather than the untouchable, the tangible over the intangible. "He took what they handed him and made it into an idol cast in the shape of a calf, fashioning it with a tool. Then they said, 'These are your gods, Israel, who brought you up out of Egypt'" (Ex. 32:4).

What was so appealing about that calf? They could *touch* this "god;" they didn't have to have faith to know it was there. They could *see* this "god;" they had probably seen one like it in Egypt—it was *familiar* territory. We almost always prefer the familiar to the unfamiliar. They preferred this idol because they could touch it, see it, and were familiar with it.

What were the results of this idolatry and loss of focus? Jack Hayford does a masterful job illustrating what happened in his video series, *Worship His Majesty*. I suggest you pick up a copy of the videos or the companion book. The results of this loss of focus were devastating. When Moses came down the mountain and saw what the people had done, he asked the people, "Who is on the Lord's side?"[54] Only the tribe of Levi responded. So then, the Levites took the place of God's original design for the entire nation, which was:

> Then Moses went up to God, and the Lord called to him from the mountain and said, "This is what you are to say to the descendants of Jacob and what you are to tell the people of Israel: 'You yourselves have seen what I did to Egypt, and how I carried you

---

[54] Ex. 32:26

on eagles' wings and brought you to myself. Now if you obey me fully and keep my covenant, then out of all nations you will be my treasured possession. Although the whole earth is mine, you will be for me *a kingdom of priests and a holy nation.'* These are the words you are to speak to the Israelites."

(Ex. 19:3–6, italics mine)

God's original blueprint for the Israelites was for them to be a *kingdom of priests* unto God. But because of their loss of focus, because of their rebellion, only one tribe—the Levites—became priests. God's original intention for the Church is the same: "To him who loves us and has freed us from our sins by his blood, and has made us to be a kingdom and priests to serve his God and Father—to him be glory and power for ever and ever! Amen" (Rev. 1:5–6). And, "You have made them to be a kingdom and priests to serve our God, and they will reign on the earth" (Rev. 5:10). In our carnal and immature thinking we have allowed pastors and staff ministers to take the place of the whole congregation being priests. I guess some of us also look for someone *to take on the bulk of the responsibility so that we can be free from it.* I wonder if some of us don't want to be a kingdom of priests either. We don't want to *do* ministry. That isn't our focus.

As mentioned earlier, one of the reasons they made

a calf is it was familiar. Please note: *although God had removed them from Egypt, Egypt had not been removed from them.* Somehow, they constantly thought Egypt was better, preferable in some way:

> The Israelites said to them, "If only we had died by the Lord's hand in Egypt! There we sat around pots of meat and ate all the food we wanted, but you have brought us out into this desert to starve this entire assembly to death."
>
> (Ex. 16:3)

> But the people were thirsty for water there, and they grumbled against Moses. They said, "Why did you bring us up out of Egypt to make us and our children and livestock die of thirst?"
>
> (Ex. 17:3)

Most of us would not admit to it publicly—especially not in church—but sometimes we think our life in sin was more "fun." No restrictions. No rules. No judgmental eyes. No early curfew on Saturday night. It looked fun; it appeared appealing; but it was slavery all the same. Be warned: "It is for freedom that Christ has set us free. Stand firm, then, and do not let yourselves be burdened again by a yoke of slavery" (Gal. 5:1). Don't lose your focus!

Postponed Promise

I am suggesting one can postpone what God has for them; they can delay God's best for them. When one acts carnally, God cannot bless; not "will not"—cannot! It is much like the problem Jesus had in his hometown.

> Jesus said to them, "A prophet is not without honor except in his own town, among his relatives and in his own home." He *could not do* any miracles there, except lay his hands on a few sick people and heal them. He was amazed at their lack of faith.
>
> (MK. 6:4–6, ITALICS MINE)

The Israelites showed their carnal and immature ways: (1) by grumbling, (2) by not following God's chosen leaders, (3) by losing their focus and erecting an idol, and finally, (4) by not expressing God-honoring faith in taking the Promised Land. I realize I am skipping quite a lot. There may be events between the golden calf and Kadesh Barnea that you wish I would cover, but I want to move to their spying-out the land before trying to enter.

When they arrived at Kadesh Barnea, Moses sent twelve spies into the land (at the people's request) to check out the inhabitants.[55] Ten of the twelve spies came back

---

[55] Deut. 1:19

with a bad report and discouraged the people. Let's read Moses' summary of what happened at Kadesh Barnea:

> "But you were unwilling to go up; you rebelled against the command of the Lord your God. You *grumbled* in your tents and said, '*The Lord hates us*; so he brought us out of Egypt to deliver us into the hands of the Amorites to destroy us.'"
>
> (DEUT. 1:26–27, ITALICS MINE)

Allow me to paraphrase: God said, "Go up and possess." The people grumbled and said, "The Lord hates us." So God said, "Then forget the whole deal."[56] *Whoa! Forget the Promised Land? I don't think so! Let's go up and possess.*

> Then you replied, "We have sinned against the Lord. We will go up and fight, as the Lord our God commanded us." So every one of you put on his weapons, thinking it easy to go up into the hill country.
>
> But the Lord said to me, "Tell them, 'Do not go up and fight, because I will not be with you. You will be defeated by your enemies.'"
>
> So I told you, but you would not listen. You rebelled against the Lord's command and in your

---

[56] Deut. 1:42

arrogance you marched up into the hill country. The Amorites who lived in those hills came out against you; they chased you like a swarm of bees and beat you down from Seir all the way to Hormah.

(DEUT. 1:41–44)

As I wrote earlier, questioning God ultimately leads to disobeying God. Their actions here proved that principle to be true. They were acting carnally. Acting out of the flesh rather than faith leads to defeat. The major problem was the people were not faith-filled. When God spoke, they did not believe and rebelled. NOTE: When God tells you to do something, do it. Don't wait until you feel like it or you may be going without his blessing. The Israelites tried to go up when they wanted—even against a further word from God—and were soundly defeated. Further, their lack of faith postponed the promise.

After this, it was another thirty-eight years[57] before they would again attempt to enter the land! And at that point, every man above twenty years of age (except Caleb and Joshua) had died in the desert. Disobedience leads to death even for a one-time believer. (They all slayed a lamb and went through the sea, didn't they?) God never intended for this to be a long journey. He gave them a chance to enter at Kadesh Barnea, but sin kept them

---

[57] They spent over a year at Sinai building the Tabernacle and its articles.

in the desert. Read the opening verses to the Book of Deuteronomy:

> These are the words Moses spoke to all Israel in the wilderness east of the Jordan—that is, in the Arabah—opposite Suph, between Paran and Tophel, Laban, Hazeroth and Dizahab. (It takes eleven days to go from Horeb to Kadesh Barnea by the Mount Seir road.)
>
> (DEUT. 1:1–2)

Eleven days! And they turned it into forty years! Talk about a postponed promise!

Sin kept them living carnally and immaturely. Sin keeps us from making spiritual progress too. God wanted them to have a victorious life, but they were not a faith-filled people. God wants us to have a victorious life as well. How are *we* doing?

During July 25–28, 1996, Joyce Meyer, the noted TV Bible teacher, shared ten principles of what she called a "Wilderness Mentality." I share her thoughts here as fodder for further meditation:

#1 – "My future is based on my past and my present."
#2 – "Someone do it for me; I don't want to take the responsibility."

#3 – "Please make everything easy. I can't take it if things are too hard."

#4 – "Grumbling, faultfinding, and complaining"

#5 – "Don't make me wait for anything; I deserve everything immediately."

#6 – "My behavior may be wrong, but it's not my fault."

#7 – "Self-pity"

#8 – "I don't deserve God's blessings because I am not worthy."

#9 – "Jealousy, envy, and comparison."

#10 – "I'm going to do it my way or not at all."[58]

To review the sermon notes in their entirety, please visit the link in the footnote.

We have quickly surveyed the major problems in the wilderness. To fully understand what happened in the desert, we need to look at the New Testament's interpretation of those events. We will begin with the third chapter of Hebrews which addresses the plight of the children of Israel while journeying in the desert: "Therefore, holy brothers and sisters, who share in the heavenly calling, fix your thoughts on Jesus, whom we acknowledge as our apostle and high priest" (Heb. 3:1). When we looked at the

---

[58] Joyce Meyer, "Wilderness Mentality," Joyce Meyer Ministries, accessed August 31, 2017, http://www.jmmindia.org/JMMSITE/jmm/ministries/Teaching%20Notes/TN25%20-%20WILDERNESS%20MENTALITY.pdf.

sin involving the golden calf, we noted the major problem was a lack of focus. Here, the writer of Hebrews encourages his readers to focus *on Jesus*. Hebrews also states:

> So, as the Holy Spirit says: "Today, if you hear his voice, do not harden your hearts as you did in the rebellion, during *the time of testing in the wilderness*, where your ancestors tested and tried me, though for forty years they saw what I did. That is why I was angry with that generation; and I said, 'Their hearts are always going astray, and they have not known my ways.' So I declared on oath in my anger, 'They shall never enter my rest.'"
>
> (HEB. 3:7–11, ITALICS MINE)

Further, he wrote:

> Who were they who heard and rebelled? Were they not all those Moses led out of Egypt? And with whom was he angry for forty years? Was it not with those who sinned, whose *bodies fell in the wilderness*? And to whom did God swear that they would never enter his rest if not to those who *disobeyed*? So we see that they were not able to enter, because of their *unbelief*.
>
> (HEB. 3:16–19, ITALICS MINE)

Read those verses again. The writer says, *many die* remaining in the state of carnality and immaturity. They never get to the place of *victorious living*. They never get to the *Promised Land*. The implication should not be missed; some have a good start but fail to finish well. All those who *fell in the wilderness* (Heb. 3:17) had applied the blood of the lamb to the doorposts of their houses and had gone through the water of the Red Sea on dry ground. And yet, they never made it to the best God had for them—they died in the desert of carnality.

A very familiar NT example is Ananias and Sapphira.[59] There is absolutely no indication that they were anything other than true converts to Christ. But their carnal thinking—wanting to be seen as more sacrificial than they really were—caused their deaths (like in the wilderness).

We also can view authentic believers in Corinth having carnal thinking and actions.

So then, whoever eats the bread or drinks the cup of the Lord in an unworthy manner will be guilty of sinning against the body and blood of the Lord. Everyone ought to examine themselves before they eat of the bread and drink from the cup. For those who eat and drink without discerning the body of Christ eat and drink judgment on themselves. That

---

[59] Acts 5:1–11

is why many among you are weak and sick, and a number of you have fallen asleep. But if we were more discerning with regard to ourselves, we would not come under such judgment. Nevertheless, when we are judged by the Lord, we are being disciplined so that we will not be condemned with the world.

(1 COR. 11:27–32)

"Fallen asleep" is a euphemism for "dying." Believers were dying (like in the desert) because they ate the Lord's Supper in an "unworthy manner"? Yes, that is what those verses are saying. What is an "unworthy manner"? Eating without regard for one's personal holiness.

Returning to the Book of Hebrews for a moment:

By faith the people passed through the Red Sea as on dry land; but when the Egyptians tried to do so, they were drowned.

By faith the walls of Jericho fell, after the army had marched around them for seven days.

(HEB. 11:29–30)

In that great chapter of faith, often called the "Faith Hall of Fame," the writer recounted the remarkable events of the Exodus. I hate to make an argument from silence, but please notice what the writer did not say. He jumped from the victory at the Red Sea to the victory at Jericho—completely skipping the journeying years. Why? Because they showed such little faith.

Before moving to the next chapter, there is one more thing we need to briefly consider. During their time in the wilderness, the Israelites were accompanied—actually, led—by a pillar of cloud by day and a pillar of fire by night. When the pillar moved, the Israelites broke camp and followed it; when it rested, the Israelites set up camp. They were continuously led by this *external* manifestation of the Holy Spirit. I mention this here for two reasons: First, it was part of the journey in the wilderness; and second, it is a type of being led by the Holy Spirit. Amazing! Even in their carnality, they could still be led by the Holy Spirit! We will return to this idea in the next chapter.

Excursus

"A rose by any other name would smell as sweet" is a popular reference to a line in William Shakespeare's play *Romeo and Juliet*. The reference is often used to imply that the names of things do not affect what they really are.[60] May I turn that phrase? "Excrement by any other name

---

[60] "A rose by any other name would smell as sweet," Wikipedia, September 24, 2019, accessed November 19, 2018, https://en.wikipedia.org/wiki/A_rose_by_any_other_name_would_smell_as_sweet.

would smell as foul." I think we can all agree to call *poop*[61] a flower doesn't make it so.

Suppose we switched the names of rose and poop around. Changing their names will not change their material characteristics. To call something by a different name does not change what it is in reality. If we did what I suggested, would anyone want to smell my rose? I don't think so! This is essential to understand the principle I am going to present. The objects retain their respective qualities, their respective characteristics.

You can call a flower *poop*, but it still smells like a flower; you can call poop a *flower,* but it still smells like poop. I try to be courteous to those who are next to use the bathroom; I use air freshener. Surprisingly, my wife doesn't like it when I do so. She says, "All you do is make nasty-smelling poop into sweet-smelling poop, but it still smells like poop." She has a point. You can use a mask to cover up something or change its name, but it retains its nature; its basic features don't change. It is imperative to understand that principle because of what the Israelites did.

What I would like us to consider at this juncture is

---

[61] For those who feel this is an inappropriate word to use, let me ask a few questions. Have you ever heard someone say, "My baby has excrement in his diaper"? No? How about hearing a parent exclaim, "The baby had a bowel movement"? Probably not. What you have heard most parents say is, "The baby has a poopy diaper."

the way the Israelites—fresh out of slavery—viewed their God. Who was this God who had rescued them? What kind of God was he? What did he look like? We need to return to Exodus chapter 32:

> When the people saw that Moses was so long in coming down from the mountain, they gathered around Aaron and said, "Come, make us gods who will go before us. As for this fellow Moses who brought us up out of Egypt, we don't know what has happened to him."
>
> Aaron answered them, "Take off the gold earrings that your wives, your sons and your daughters are wearing, and bring them to me." So all the people took off their earrings and brought them to Aaron. He took what they handed him and made it into an idol cast in the shape of a calf, fashioning it with a tool. Then they said, "These are your gods, Israel, who brought you up out of Egypt."
>
> (Ex. 32:1–4)

This story from the history of the Israelites is incredulous! How could any people so quickly turn their backs on the God who saved them from a life of slavery? Or did they? In their minds, they hadn't. Did you catch it? Did you see how the Israelites violated the principle we have established? They made an idol and then called it *a god*;

more than that, they said, "These are your gods...who brought you up out of Egypt." Did they turn from YHWH or *simply* try to attribute to an idol the characteristics of the living God? But it was still an idol, wasn't it?

They were doing what many today do without giving it a second's thought. They call an idol by another name and feel justified to offer it veneration or worship. When I right click on *veneration*, then left click on synonyms, one of the results my word processor provides is *worship*. Is veneration another one of those words? "A rose by any other name...." If veneration is substantially worship, are those who venerate violating scripture?

When Jesus battled Satan in the wilderness, he gave him the following response to his request for worship. Jesus said to him, "Away from me, Satan! For it is written: 'Worship the Lord your God, and serve him only'" (Matt. 4:10).[62] "Worship the Lord your God...only." For such a small word only has a great impact. In this context, I would think Jesus meant (1) don't worship idols (Ex. 34:17; 1 Jn. 5:21); (2) don't worship angels (Col. 2:18; Rev. 19:9–10); and (3) don't worship anything that has been created (Rom. 1:25).

Some modern religions have called worship by a different name and called idols by a different name and

---

[62] Also Luke 4:8

duped millions (including themselves). They seem to be ignorant of what they are doing. God help us all!

Discipleship Challenge

As difficult to write as the previous chapter was, this one was worse. Why? It got too personal. As I worked through the plight of the Israelites, I realized I have lived most of my Christian life in the wilderness, not the Promised Land. Too often—and still—I find myself having "wilderness thinking," immature, carnal thinking. Ouch!

As we can see by the events of the Old Testament as well as the understanding of the New Testament, the Israelites lived a *defeated lifestyle*. The wilderness was meant to be a path, not a destination. It was a place they were to camp, not settle. They were not *following* as close to the Lord as they should have. They were not as *focused* on the Lord but looked for a substitute. They were not *faith-filled* but rather fear-filled. When we contemplate the events outlined in this chapter, we should feel awful. Look how many multiplied thousands of Israelites started the journey well but never finished—they died in the desert. That should bother us, because the same thing still happens daily in the Church of the Risen Savior. Every day, people die without ever reaching God's best for them in this life. They are satisfied to live in the desert. What about you? Are you settling?

As much as the Israelites wanted to follow the Lord, their faith was too weak. Their faith (or fear of Pharaoh) was enough to get them through the Red Sea, but it was not strong enough to encourage them to follow YHWH out of love and gratitude. They perfectly foreshadowed the *carnal* Christian life.

Many today within the church are in a similar state— they have accepted the Lord and his atoning sacrifice, they have gone through the waters of baptism, and yet they seem to live a defeated Christian life! What gives? What's the answer? Read the following slowly: "That…answer… is…in…the…next…chapter."

PART THREE

THE JOURNEY INTO PROMISE

CHAPTER 5

THE JORDAN RIVER

An Empowerment

F inally! After forty years of traveling around in the *same* desert, the Israelites once again came to the border of the Promised Land. The only thing between them and a promise fulfilled was the Jordan River—at flood stage.[63]

The Jordan River is the shadow we must come to understand in this chapter and in the life of a disciple. Before I offer my opinion, let us consider the traditional understanding of this shadow—the Jordan River has been understood historically as representing death. We see this motif in the Christian hymn "Because He Lives," verse 3:

---

[63] Jos. 3:15

And then one day
I'll cross the river
I'll fight life's final war with pain
And then as death
Gives way to victory
I'll see the lights
Of glory and
I'll know he lives[64]

The hymnal the church used when I first preached this message agrees with this interpretation as can be seen in the hymn "On Jordan's Stormy Banks."

On Jordan's stormy banks I stand, and cast a
    wishful eye
To Canaan's fair and happy land, where my
    possessions lie.
All o'er those wide extended plains shines one
    eternal day;
There God the Son forever reigns and scatters
    night away.
No chilling winds nor pois'nous breath can reach
    that healthful shore;

---

[64] William J. Gaither and Gloria Gaither, "Because He Lives" (CMG Song# 3054) Copyright © 1983 Hanna Street Music (BMI) adm. at CapitolCMGPublishing.com)

Sickness and sorrow, pain and death are felt and
feared no more.[65]

That hymn looks across the Jordan to heaven, the
Promised Land. As the author placed himself on the
shore of the Jordan, he saw only death between him and
his heavenly reward, his long awaited promise. Victor
Hoven shared many years ago in *Shadow and Substance*:
"The Jordan was…a type of death through which the
Christian passes by divine guidance and help into the
heavenly rest (Ps. 23:4)."[66] And finally, our most noted
stance comes from the pen of John Bunyan. In his book,
Pilgrim's Progress, he pictured the Jordan River as that
which is crossed in order to get to the Celestial City—i.e.,
heaven.

> When Mr. Standfast had thus set things in order, and
> the time being come for him to haste him away, he also
> went down to the river. Now there was a great calm at
> that time in the river; wherefore Mr. Standfast, when
> he was about half-way in, stood a while, and talked
> with his companions that had waited upon him thither.
> And he said, "This river has been a terror to many; yea,
> the thoughts of it also have often frightened me; but

---

[65] Samuel Stennett, "On Jordan's Stormy Banks," Public Domain.

[66] Hoven, p. 57.

now methinks I stand easy; my foot is fixed upon that on which the feet of the priests that bore the ark of the covenant stood while Israel went over Jordan (Joshua 3:17). The waters indeed are to the palate bitter, and to the stomach cold; yet the thoughts of what I am going to, and of the convoy that waits for me on the other side, do lie as a glowing coal at my heart. I see myself now at the end of my journey; my toilsome days are ended. I am going to see that head which was crowned with thorns, and that face which was spit upon for me. I have formerly lived by hearsay and faith; but now I go where I shall live by sight, and shall be with Him in whose company I delight myself."[67]

As can be seen by these hymns and books, the traditional, historical understanding of the representation of crossing the Jordan River is that of death. Many interpret it this way because they also see the Promised Land as a shadow of heaven.

Whereas the traditional view of crossing the Jordan is a representation of one's death, I believe crossing the Jordan River is a shadow of the *baptism with the Holy Spirit*. There are several reasons why I believe this is true.

[67] John Bunyan, *The Harvard Classics: The Pilgrim's Progress*, (Danbury, CT: Grolier Enterprises, 1980), p. 317.

First, if crossing the Red Sea on dry ground represented a baptism (1 Cor. 10:2), then this crossing should also be a type of baptism. Since we are to be baptized in water only once, this baptism must represent something different in the life of a disciple. There are only two other baptisms mentioned in the NT, a baptism with the Holy Spirit (Acts 1:5) and a baptism of suffering (Mk. 10:38–39). I believe the former makes better sense in this context than the latter. By the way, the Jordan River overflowing represents the abundance of the Holy Spirit.

Second, something happened at the Jordan that gave the Israelites "power." Something big happened there! Note how different the people were after crossing.

BEFORE the Jordan, they journeyed.
AFTER the Jordan, they settled.

BEFORE the Jordan, they lived fearful lives.
AFTER the Jordan, they lived fearless lives.

BEFORE the Jordan, they only had tablets of stone.
AFTER the Jordan, they had a testimony in stone.

BEFORE the Jordan, they were victims.
AFTER the Jordan, they were victors.

A third reason is found in the words of Jesus as he stood up to speak at the Feast of Tabernacles in Jerusalem approximately six months before his crucifixion.

> On the last and greatest day of the festival, Jesus stood and said in a loud voice, "Let anyone who is thirsty come to me and drink. Whoever believes in me, as Scripture has said, *rivers of living water will flow from within them." By this he meant the Spirit*, whom those who believed in him were later to receive. Up to that time the Spirit had not been given, since Jesus had not yet been glorified.
>
> (JN. 7:37–39, ITALICS MINE)

Jesus made the connection between a river and the Holy Spirit. I have recently noticed the quotation Jesus referenced was really about himself! Look at verse 38 again, closely. He first said, "Whoever believes in me." He made a direct connection for the NT believer to have faith in him to receive the Spirit. Next, he said, "As the Scripture has said." This is Jesus making reference in scripture to a person, which I believe is himself. Finally, he quoted (or paraphrased)[68] "Rivers of living water will flow from within him." Most often the word "him" has been understood to be the believer, but the quotation makes more

---

[68] Isa. 44:3

sense if it refers to Jesus from whom the Spirit comes. In other words, the streams of living water flow from within Jesus to the believer. Verse 39 agrees with this as it mentions that the believers were to "receive" the Spirit, not distribute it—a fact mentioned in Revelation 22:1 as well: "Then the angel showed me the river of the water of life, as clear as crystal, flowing from the throne of God and of the Lamb."

The fourth reason I believe the crossing of the Jordan River represents the baptism with the Holy Spirit is the Spirit's association with the Jordan River in the lives of Elijah and Elisha.

Fifty men of the company of the prophets went and stood at a distance, facing the place where Elijah and Elisha had stopped at the Jordan. Elijah took his cloak, rolled it up and struck the water with it. The water divided to the right and to the left, and the two of them crossed over on dry ground.

When they had crossed, Elijah said to Elisha, "Tell me, what can I do for you before I am taken from you?"

"Let me inherit a double portion of your spirit," Elisha replied.

"You have asked a difficult thing," Elijah said,

"yet if you see me when I am taken from you, it will be yours—otherwise, it will not."

As they were walking along and talking together, suddenly a chariot of fire and horses of fire appeared and separated the two of them, and Elijah went up to heaven in a whirlwind. Elisha saw this and cried out, "My father! My father! The chariots and horsemen of Israel!" And Elisha saw him no more. Then he took hold of his garment and tore it in two.

Elisha then picked up Elijah's cloak that had fallen from him and went back and stood on the bank of the Jordan. He took the cloak that had fallen from Elijah and struck the water with it. "Where now is the Lord, the God of Elijah?" he asked. When he struck the water, it divided to the right and to the left, and he crossed over.

The company of the prophets from Jericho, who were watching, said, "The spirit of Elijah is resting on Elisha." And they went to meet him and bowed to the ground before him.

(2 KIN. 2:7–15)

The final reason I believe crossing the Jordan represents the baptism with the Holy Spirit is neither the pillar of cloud nor the pillar of fire (both types of the Holy Spirit) is mentioned as present. During their wilderness journey, both were mentioned as present and leading the way.

> By day the Lord went ahead of them in a pillar of cloud to guide them on their way and by night in a pillar of fire to give them light, so that they could travel by day or night. Neither the pillar of cloud by day nor the pillar of fire by night left its place in front of the people.
>
> (Ex. 13:21–22)

Once the Israelites crossed the Jordan, the cloud and fire are no longer mentioned. By this, we are shown the transformation that takes place when a believer is baptized with the Holy Spirit. He is not just led by the Spirit but is full of the Spirit. The believer is not just led by the Spirit, he is ready for…. (We will save the end of that sentence for the next chapter.) Another has said in reference to Jesus' water baptism by John at the Jordan, "The Jordan has now become the place of new beginnings."[69]

The text we need to examine to better understand the historicity of this shadow is Joshua 3:14–4:7.

> So when the people broke camp to cross the Jordan, the priests carrying the ark of the covenant went

---

[69] Estelle, p. 217

ahead of them. Now the Jordan is at flood stage all during harvest. Yet as soon as the priests who carried the ark reached the Jordan and their feet touched the water's edge, the water from upstream stopped flowing. It piled up in a heap a great distance away, at a town called Adam in the vicinity of Zarethan, while the water flowing down to the Sea of the Arabah (that is, the Dead Sea) was completely cut off. So the people crossed over opposite Jericho. The priests who carried the ark of the covenant of the Lord stopped in the middle of the Jordan and stood on dry ground, while all Israel passed by until the whole nation had completed the crossing on dry ground.

When the whole nation had finished crossing the Jordan, the Lord said to Joshua, "Choose twelve men from among the people, one from each tribe, and tell them to take up twelve stones from the middle of the Jordan, from right where the priests are standing, and carry them over with you and put them down at the place where you stay tonight."

So Joshua called together the twelve men he had appointed from the Israelites, one from each tribe, and said to them, "Go over before the ark of the Lord your God into the middle of the Jordan. Each of you is to take up a stone on his shoulder, according to the number of the tribes of the Israelites, to serve as a sign among you. In the future, when your children ask you, 'What do these stones mean?' tell them that the flow of the Jordan was cut off before the ark of the covenant of the Lord. When it crossed the Jordan, the waters of the Jordan were cut off. These stones are to be a memorial to the people of Israel forever."

(Jos. 3:14–4:7)

Crossing the Jordan River and being filled with the Holy Spirit have several things in common. (I will use the terms "baptized with" and "filled with" interchangeably— see Excursus below.) First, the Israelites had to enter the water by faith. And in this, the spiritual leaders had to take the first step. I have never been beside a river that is at flood stage, but I have seen plenty of television coverage on the news to get the idea—you don't want to get caught in the current. By their action, prompted by faith, they were asking God to keep his end of the bargain. The same paradigm exists for those who wish to receive the Holy Spirit; you must wade in with faith and expect God to keep his word.

According to the Gospel of Luke, there is a second thing we must do to receive the Holy Spirit—ask!

"So I say to you: Ask and it will be given to you; seek and you will find; knock and the door will be opened to you. For everyone who asks receives; the one who seeks finds; and to the one who knocks, the door will be opened.

"Which of you fathers, if your son asks for a fish, will give him a snake instead? Or if he asks for an egg, will give him a scorpion? If you then, though you are evil, know how to give good gifts to your children, how much more will your Father in heaven give the Holy Spirit to those who ask him!"

(Lk. 11:9–13)

You must have faith and you must ask.

Third, they had to enter without Moses. (Remember, Moses is a shadow picture of Christ.) You might recall Moses did not enter the Promised Land but died on a mountain (Nebo) on the eastern shore of the Jordan. "And Moses the servant of the Lord died there in Moab, as the Lord had said. He buried him in Moab, in the valley opposite Beth Peor, but to this day no one knows where his grave is" (Deut. 34:5–6). Moses' absence was a fore-shadowing of Jesus' departure back to heaven before the disciples were filled with the Spirit. "But very truly I tell you, it is for your good that I am going away. Unless I go away, the Advocate will not come to you; but if I go,

I will send him to you" (Jn. 16:7). Above, we looked at the life of Elijah. Near the end of his ministry, he chose a replacement named Elisha. I ask you, at what point in the ministry of Elisha (the replacement) did he receive power from God? It was after the departure of Elijah and passing back through the Jordan River (and please note: when he returned to begin his ministry, Elijah did not go with him). Elijah, upon his ascension, let his mantle fall upon his disciple, Elisha. Jesus, upon his ascension, let his "mantle," the Holy Spirit, fall upon his twelve disciples on the Day of Pentecost. Do you see the pattern? Moses (a shadow of Christ) was absent from the Israelites when they crossed over to the Promised Land; Elijah was taken from Elisha before Elisha received God's power; in the New Testament, Jesus ascended before Pentecost.

Fourth, they were to use this moment as a memorial—a testimony to what God had done. As the Israelites crossed over, Joshua chose twelve men—one from each tribe—to pick up a stone from the middle of the dry riverbed to build a memorial. Note: When they went through the Jordan, they picked up twelve stones from the midst of it, not twelve stones from the wilderness, to be their testimony. God wanted their testimony to be what happened at the river, not what happened in the desert. He wants this for us also.

Look what Joshua did with those twelve stones:

Joshua set up the twelve stones that had been in the middle of the Jordan at the spot where the priests who carried the ark of the covenant had stood. And they are there to this day.

(Jos. 4:9)

I expected him to build an altar and offer a sacrifice, but no, he stands them up.

Standing stones were used to mark graves (Gen. 35:20), mark out a place of divine revelation (Gen. 35:14; Ex. 24:4), used to announce royal legislation, and to mark military victories.[70]

The main purpose of these stones was to be a testimony! May I suggest the main purpose for being filled with the Holy Spirit is so we can have a testimony also? In *Empowered Evangelicals*, the author quoted R.A. Torrey: "This 'baptism with the Spirit,' according to Torrey, 'always imparts power in service' and 'boldness in testimony.'"[71] Reflect on the following episodes from the Book of Acts: "But you will receive power when the Holy Spirit comes

---

[70] Neil Asher Silberman, *Biblical Archeology Review*, March/April 1989, Vol. XV, No. 2, pp. 58–59.

[71] Rich Nathan and Ken Wilson, *Empowered Evangelicals: Bringing Together the Best of the Evangelical and Charismatic Worlds*, (Boise: Ampelon Publishing, 2009, p. 158.

on you; and *you will be my witnesses* in Jerusalem, and in all Judea and Samaria, and to the ends of the earth" (Acts 1:8, italics mine). In Acts 4:13, Peter and John were before the Sanhedrin: "When they saw the courage of Peter and John and realized that they were unschooled, ordinary men, they were astonished and they took note that these men had been with Jesus." Isn't this the same Peter who denied Christ three times before he was filled with the Spirit? Yes, it is. Many claim Peter was emboldened by the resurrection, but one never sees him boldly standing for Jesus before he was filled with the Holy Spirit. On their release, Peter and John went back to their own people and reported all the chief priests and elders had said to them.

> When they heard this, they raised their voices together in prayer to God....
>
> After they prayed, the place *where they were meeting was shaken. And they were all filled with the Holy Spirit and spoke the word of God boldly."*
> (ACTS 4:24 AND 31, ITALICS MINE)

They spoke the word of God boldly (i.e., they testified of what God had done through Jesus Christ).

Let's Get Practical

We often do not seek the baptism of the Spirit because of three reasons: ignorance, fear and apathy.

Because we are promised the Holy Spirit at our conversion (Acts 2:38), many do not realize they must seek it. We are ignorant of this responsibility. Please reread Luke 11:9–13 above. It says to ask, seek, and knock.

The second reason is fear. Many mainline and evangelical Christians are afraid of what may happen if they fully let the Holy Spirit have his way and are "baptized with the Holy Spirit." No doubt, these have heard "horror" stories about the odd things that happen under such circumstances: people losing control of their emotions and praising God too exuberantly for their taste. Maybe they have heard of people rolling on the floors—after all, "holy rollers" had to come from somewhere! Others have heard of people speaking ecstatically—i.e., in tongues. They fear these demonstrations because (1) they are not familiar with these forms of worship, and (2) they are uncomfortable with such manifestations. *If that is what the Holy Spirit is going to make me do, then I will settle for the sealing of the Spirit[72] at salvation, thank you.* It is a shame we

---

[72] 2 Cor. 1:21–22

often let fear rule our lives rather than faith. (Sounds like we are back in the wilderness.)

Another reason Christians do not seek being baptized with the Holy Spirit is lack of hunger, apathy. When was the last time you could echo the author of Psalm 42? "My soul thirsts for God, for the living God. When can I go and meet with God?" (Ps. 42:2). Many want to be Christians as "fire insurance," but really don't desire "the fire of God" in their bones,[73] for God to be in control. Therefore we are *not* hungry for the things of God.

I was taught if I chow down on junk food all the time, I will not be hungry when offered a nice juicy steak, baked potato smothered in butter, sour cream, cheese, and bacon bits, and a side order of corn or beans. When we think about it, we know which is better and more fulfilling. BUT the junk food is more convenient. You can take a bite here, travel with it there. If you were to sit down and think about it or wait until you were really hungry, I believe you would choose a steak over a Twinkie. Is talking about food making you hungry? It should! And talking about the things of the Spirit should make you hungry for the genuine thing instead of the "junk food" we have been putting in our systems.

The devil and life have our attention on temporal comforts. See if the following list of spiritual "junk food" strikes home with you:

---

[73] Jer. 20:9

- homes
- jobs
- love interests
- kids
- sports
- hobbies
- clubs
- church activities
- entertainment

These are all good in their place, BUT they only give temporary satisfaction. We need something deeper. We need empowerment. We need to be filled with the Holy Spirit!

Allow me to make several suggestions to improve your "diet." Study what the scriptures (especially, Acts) say about the filling of the Holy Spirit (the "Excursus" below is a good place to start). One of our problems is spiritual immaturity. When we were emotionally immature, we needed guidance from our parents—"Don't eat that before dinner; you will spoil your appetite." Now that we are grown, we need someone to help with our spiritual hunger—hence this chapter. You will never desire the things of God if you fill your life full of the list above (or make your own list).

We need to believe God wants to give us his all and

his best. If we believe God is holding back something we need, we will begin to doubt that he is good and we will not trust him. This is the original error of mankind. Because Adam and Eve distrusted God's goodness and thought he was holding the best back from them, they acted according to the advice of the serpent. They sinned, and therefore did not receive God's best. When we do not step out in faith, we fail to receive God's best. His best for the Israelites was the Promised Land. They had to receive it by faith. Remember, the priests had to step out in faith and enter the river at flood-stage before they could get what God promised. "And without faith it is impossible to please God..." (Heb. 11:6).

Another thing we must do is realize we have a choice: live a carnal or immature Christian life (which we talked about in the last chapter) or live the victorious Christian life having been empowered by the Holy Spirit. The Bible is replete with choices. Here is an example: "Do not get drunk on wine, which leads to debauchery. Instead, be filled with the Spirit..." (Eph. 5:18).

Many Christians do not realize one is to pray that God would give him all he needs to be his witness. A verse which we read earlier states, "If you then, though you are evil, know how to give good gifts to your children, how much more will your Father in heaven give the Holy Spirit to those who ask him!" (Lk. 11:13).

Finally, don't be satisfied with just a little; become a "bottomless cup" Christian. When I go out to eat, I like to go to the restaurants with the "bottomless cup" policy. I order and pay for only one cup of coffee, but the server makes sure it is never empty. In fact, if she or he is a good server, they will try to keep it full. Don't settle for being a "half-full" Christian.

As the nation of Israel stood on the flooded banks, they had to make a decision. You do too. Be filled with the Holy Spirit or miss out on God's best. As we will see in the next chapter, something happened at the Jordan; something that gave the Israelites the power to become victorious. Something can happen to us also; something that can give us the power to become victorious Christians—the baptism with the Holy Spirit.

Excursus

I have used the phrase "baptism with the Holy Spirit" liberally throughout this chapter. According to the New Testament, what does it mean to be "baptized with the Holy Spirit"? I find it interesting that, for all the publicity the phrase gets from our Pentecostal brothers and sisters, it is rarely used outside the gospels. The gospel accounts—which have John the Baptist as the speaker in each case—are as follows:

- "I baptize you with water for repentance. But after me comes one who is more powerful than I, whose sandals I am not worthy to carry. He will baptize you with the Holy Spirit and fire." (Matt. 3:11)
- And this was his message: "After me comes the one more powerful than I, the straps of whose sandals I am not worthy to stoop down and untie. I baptize you with water, but he will baptize you with the Holy Spirit." (Mk. 1:7–8)
- John answered them all, "I baptize you with water. But one who is more powerful than I will come, the straps of whose sandals I am not worthy to untie. He will baptize you with the Holy Spirit and fire." (Lk. 3:16)
- "And I myself did not know him, but the one who sent me to baptize with water told me, 'The man on whom you see the Spirit come down and remain is the one who will baptize with the Holy Spirit.' I have seen and I testify that this is God's Chosen One." (Jn. 1:33–34)

Outside the gospels, it is used in the following places:

- "For John baptized with water, but in a few days you will be baptized with the Holy Spirit." (Acts 1:5)
- "Then I remembered what the Lord had said:

'John baptized with water, but you will be baptized with the Holy Spirit.'" (Acts 11:16)
- A similar phrase is used in 1 Corinthians 12:13, "For we were all baptized by one Spirit so as to form one body—whether Jews or Gentiles, slave or free—and we were all given the one Spirit to drink."

In Acts 1:5, Jesus prophesied about Pentecost, which is why those who subscribe to this pattern are often called Pentecostals. In Acts 11, Peter is recalling the events which took place at the home of Cornelius the Centurion and remembers what Jesus said in Acts 1:5. The full context—which includes the verse quoted above—of what happened is:

"As I began to speak, the Holy Spirit came on them as he had come on us at the beginning. Then I remembered what the Lord had said: 'John baptized with water, but you will be baptized with the Holy Spirit.' So if God gave them the same gift as he gave us who believed in the Lord Jesus Christ, who was I to think that I could stand in God's way?"
(ACTS 11:15–17)

The third occurrence, found in 1 Corinthians 12:13, is worded differently. Whereas Acts 1:5 and 11:16 use the word *with*, 1 Corinthians 12:13 uses, *by* (NIV). But in the

Greek, *with* and *by* are the same word,[74] which could be translated to *in*.

It is always best to "let scripture interpret scripture." Therefore, we will take a survey of the way scripture interprets the "baptism with the Holy Spirit" by the use of the Bible's dynamic synonyms. Since the Book of Acts is the major concentration of those emphasizing the need for this manifestation, we will restrict our efforts within that parameter. There are a number of phrases Acts uses to describe the activity of the Holy Spirit; I hope the following chart will be helpful.

Baptized with	Come on /upon	Filled with	Poured out	Receive	Given/ gift of	Anointed with
1:5	1:8	2:4	1:17	2:38	8:18	10:38
11:16	8:16	4:8	1:18	8:15	10:45	
	10:44	4:31	2:33	8:17	15:8	
	11:15	9:17	10:45	8:19		
	19:6	13:9		10:47		
		13:52		19:1		

Figure 5.1

Figure 5.1 shows the dynamic equivalents used to speak of the Holy Spirit in the Book of Acts. After

[74] NT:1722: en (en); a primary preposition denoting (fixed) position (in place, time or state), and (by implication) instrumentality (medially or constructively), i.e., a relation of rest (intermediate between NT:1519 and NT:1537); "in," at, (up-) on, by, etc., (Strong, p. 28).

developing this visual, I have determined the best syn-
onym for "being baptized with the Holy Spirit" is to "be
filled with the Holy Spirit" or to "receive the Holy Spirit."
Remember, the promise was to be "baptized with" (Acts
1:5), but its fulfillment was "filled with" (Acts 2:4). They
are dynamic equivalents.

My conclusion is similar to what I recently read:

Finally, there is a growing number of people who
hail from non-charismatic evangelical backgrounds
but have adopted certain classical Pentecostal prac-
tices such as healing the sick, casting out demons, and
receiving prophetic revelations. Many of these people
(we are among them) believe that the so-called 'baptism in the Holy Spirit' happens at conversion and
is not a second work of grace subsequent to the new
birth. They also believe the gift of tongues is simply one
of many spiritual gifts and not the only evidence of a
particular spiritual experience."[75]

I was saved while attending a Pentecostal church; I am
forever grateful for that small body of believers. I left that
group—not because they did not love me (They did!)—
but because their doctrine and their praxis didn't seem
to match scripture. One example is "tarrying." The eleven

---

[75] Nathan and Wilson, p. 6

apostles (this was before Matthias was added in Acts 1:26) were the only ones told to tarry. "And, behold, I send the promise of my Father upon you: but tarry ye in the city of Jerusalem, until ye be endued with power from on high" (Lk. 24:49 KJV). The promise of which Jesus spoke was the Holy Spirit. Some claim that because the apostles had to tarry, so do we. But if we take the phrase in context, we would also have to do our tarrying in Jerusalem! That does not make sense for anyone but the apostles. According to the teaching I received, after one was water baptized he or she was to tarry for the Holy Spirit. One older gentleman—trying to encourage me—told me it took eleven years before he was Spirit-baptized. Eleven years! That was discouraging! What bothered me the most was it seemed so unbiblical. Where, except for the apostles (and one could argue, the Samaritans) was anyone encouraged to tarry for the Holy Spirit? And never for a lengthy time—the biblical accounts portray an immediate filling. I began a quest for a better answer. I received some relief when our church got together with another Pentecostal church for a joint service. I remember the preacher saying, "It is the sinner's responsibility to believe and repent, the church's responsibility to baptize him (in water), and God's responsibility to fill him with the Holy Spirit." I received some relief, but not an answer. To this day, I have continued to study the scriptures (not the doctrines of man) for the truth.

I am reminded of an event in my early Christianity. My first pastor (after I was saved) once said to me, "I don't know what to make of you, Brother Bill." We had been talking about how there was evidence of the Holy Spirit working in my life. He was confused. He saw the Spirit at work, yet his Pentecostal theology told him it wasn't possible since I had not been "baptized with the Holy Spirit accompanied by speaking in tongues." He could not let go of his carefully crafted theology to embrace what God was doing.

Before moving on, I want to make one thing perfectly clear: I accept as valid the testimony of those who claim to be "baptized with the Holy Spirit with the evidence of speaking in tongues." As one of my elders was wont to say, "A man with an experience is never at the mercy of a man with an argument." God is not limited in what he can do by my understanding or yours. What I don't believe is receiving the Holy Spirit with the "evidence of speaking in tongues" is (or should be) the normal experience for every Christian. Non-Pentecostals need to accept the testimony of Pentecostals as a valid, meaningful experience; Pentecostals need to accept the testimony of the non-Pentecostals—those who do not speak in tongues—as a valid, meaningful experience. Maybe our time would be better spent trying to convert the world rather than convert each other to our respective camp.

With all that said, I believe the scripture demonstrates multiple fillings of the Holy Spirit subsequent to salvation. We will use the apostle Paul for our test case. At his conversion we read:

> Then Ananias went to the house and entered it. Placing his hands on Saul, he said, "Brother Saul, the Lord—Jesus, who appeared to you on the road as you were coming here—has sent me so that you may see again and *be filled with the Holy Spirit*." Immediately, something like scales fell from Saul's eyes, and he could see again. He got up and was baptized, and after taking some food, he regained his strength.
>
> (ACTS 9:17–19, ITALICS MINE)

Later, when he began to minister as a missionary, we read, "Then Saul, who was also called Paul, *filled with the Holy Spirit*, looked straight at Elymas and said…" (Acts 13:9, italics mine). Paul was filled with the Holy Spirit (which we already comprehended in Acts 2:4 as a dynamic equivalent to being baptized with the Holy Spirit) at his conversion and later received another filling for power in ministry. This can also be demonstrated in the lives of Peter and John. Both were baptized (filled) with the Spirit on the day of Pentecost, and later, Peter was filled when addressing "the rulers, elders, and teachers of the law":

> The next day the rulers, elders and teachers of the law met in Jerusalem. Annas the high priest was there, and so were Caiaphas, John, Alexander and others of the high priest's family. They had Peter and John brought before them and began to question them: "By what power or what name did you do this?"
>
> Then Peter, filled with the Holy Spirit, said to them…
>
> (ACTS 4:5–8)

Afterward, the two were released and they gathered with the saints for prayer: "After they prayed, the place where they were meeting was shaken. And they were all filled with the Holy Spirit and spoke the word of God boldly" (Acts 4:31).

You may have noticed that "filled" in each of the scriptures above is in the past tense (aorist tense in Greek). In Greek, the aorist tense shows an action that happened at a point, but not necessarily with continued results. Some might think this is a reference to the person being filled at conversion. It seems better to understand it as a fresh filling that happened at a subsequent point for temporary empowerment for a miracle (Acts 13:9) or to witness

(Acts 4:5-8). Craig Keener in commenting on Acts 4:8 agrees with this interpretation.

> The apostles here are filled with the Holy Spirit, probably again, [973] indicating that Luke employs the language freely for empowerment for proclamation, not simply for an initial entrance into faith or empowerment (cf. 2:4; 4:31, 33)…. Although Luke speaks often of "receiving" the Spirit, he conceives of the Spirit not as simply a past possession to be commemorated but as God's powerful presence dynamically active within the community of believers.
>
> n. 973. Though "having been filled" is an aorist passive participle, it need not refer to an event as antecedent as Pentecost was; if it refers to chronology at all, it simply demands action antecedent to that of the main verb.[76]

It seems the expected normal experience for a convert is to be baptized (filled) with the Holy Spirit upon conversion and then receive subsequent fillings, as needed, for ministry.

---

[76] Craig S. Keener, Acts: *An Exegetical Commentary, Vol. 2*, (Grand Rapids: Baker Book House, 2013), p. 1144.

Discipleship Challenge

Have you, by faith, ever been baptized (filled) with the Holy Spirit in either a perceptive or non-perceptive way? What would best demonstrate that—speaking in tongues, power for ministry, or the fruit of the Spirit? If you are a follower of Jesus Christ, then you should have been baptized by the Holy Spirit at your conversion: "For we were all baptized by one Spirit so as to form one body—whether Jews or Gentiles, slave or free—and we were all given the one Spirit to drink" (1 Cor. 12:13).

Do you consciously seek subsequent fillings for ministry? As was demonstrated above, the apostles Paul, Peter, and John had fillings after their conversions for the purpose of power to minister effectively for Christ. I encourage you to seek such fillings so you can fulfill the ministry to which you have been called.

CHAPTER 6

THE PROMISED LAND

A Time for Warfare

Now, we come to the beginning! *The beginning? Isn't this the end, Bill?* I consider it the beginning because this is where my quest started. For years, I heard the ideas promoted of the types we have visited: Passover signified our sin being passed over; crossing the Red Sea represented our Christian baptism; the wilderness wandering symbolized the Christian walk of a disciple; crossing the Jordan pictured one's death; and the Promised Land denoted heaven. I wrestled with one interpretation in particular: *If the Promised Land represents heaven, why is there fighting going on? Are we going to be having conflicts after we die? Is church just a preparation for the next life, the next fight?* I say this is the beginning because that concept needed answered first. When it was, all the other types (the first five chapters) fell into place.

If the Promised Land does not represent heaven, then what does it typify in the life of the average disciple? *It is spiritual warfare.* Not until we are filled with the Holy Spirit (our Jordan experience) are we ready to take on the battles of faith. The Promised Land is not the shadow of heaven but of *the victorious Christian life* in the midst of spiritual warfare. God's destiny for us is to be victorious spiritual warriors, not cloud-riding harp players! I am not the only one to question the traditional interpretation. My mentor for ten years, Bishop Joey Johnson, believes, "For Christians, the Promised Land is abundant Christian Living."[77] My question: *How can it be abundant if we are living spiritually defeated lives?*

Is the phrase "spiritual warfare" new to you? Do you know how to do it? I was saved in 1978 at the age of twenty-five. I do not believe I ever heard that phrase for the first ten years of my Christian walk. Today there are books, conferences, and seminars about spiritual warfare. Unfortunately, I have read only a handful of the books and attended just one of the conferences. So, if you haven't

---

[77] Bishop Joey Johnson, *God Is Greater than Family Mess,* (Dallas: Saint Paul Press, 2009), p. 114.

done much study in this area, we are fellow students in this. Let this chapter be an introductory lesson into spiritual warfare.

Maybe the question arises in your mind, "What makes you think this *is* a picture of spiritual warfare?"

When the Israelites entered the land, they did not get what was promised without fighting for it. As we have seen throughout this work, what happened to them in the physical world usually has ramifications for us in the spiritual world. As Ken Abraham has written, "When you think of it, the only way you can have a victorious Christian life is by having some obstacles to overcome."[78]

I see the same thing in the life of Jesus: He passed through the waters of the Jordan (in baptism) and the Holy Spirit came upon him. He entered into the wilderness (forty-day fast and the devil's three temptations); then he went forth into spiritual battle. You have probably noticed, his entire earthly life was a clash with the invisible realm. Look how many times he cast out demons: Matthew 4:24; 8:16; 8:28–34; 9:32–34; 12:22–24; 15:22; 17:18; and that's only Matthew's account!

With that groundwork laid, let us view the specifics of the Israelites' conflicts and what applies to us today. As

---

[78] Ken Abraham, *The Disillusioned Christian: Advice for the Burned and Burned Out,* (San Bernardino, CA: Here's Life Publishers, Inc., 1991), p. 131.

we do so, keep the following in mind: (1) Their physical battles represent our spiritual battles, and (2) Joshua represents the Holy Spirit. After the Israelites crossed the Jordan we read:

> About forty thousand armed for battle crossed over before the Lord to the plains of Jericho for war.
> That day the Lord exalted Joshua in the sight of all Israel; and they stood in awe of him all the days of his life, just as they had stood in awe of Moses.
>
> (Jos. 4:13–14)

Moses was a type of Christ; Joshua was a type of the Holy Spirit (he replaced Moses) Note: (From last chapter) Joshua was not exalted until Moses left; the ministry of the Holy Spirit was not in full effect until Jesus went back to the Father. We are now ready to look at their battles.

Preparation for the Fight

There are several things they did before they fought their first battle. First, they crossed the Jordan on the tenth of the first month. This is the day the lamb was to be set aside for the Passover. As they were setting apart their lambs, God was setting them apart from the nations around them in Canaan. Second, they sent spies to Jericho. In

Lord, Is It Warfare? Teach Me to Stand, Kay Arthur has written that to defeat the enemy, one must know who the enemy is and now how the enemy acts. Third, the men were circumcised; those born in the wilderness had never been circumcised.[79] As was mentioned during the first Passover, all males must be circumcised to partake—this was a sign of repentance. This is a message to us to never neglect the daily disciplines that keep our hearts sensitive toward God. Then they celebrated the Passover on the fourteenth—what was the meaning of all this? They had to be sanctified (made holy, set apart) before they could fight a "holy war." Christian disciples are told to "Make every effort to live in peace with everyone and to be holy; without holiness no one will see the Lord" (Heb. 12:14). They also had to follow…

The Lord's Battle Plans

Joshua received his instructions from the Lord. Joshua did not attack the city by his own wisdom; he attacked the city the way the Lord instructed:

> Then the Lord said to Joshua, "See, I have delivered Jericho into your hands, along with its king and its fighting men. March around the city once with all

---

[79] Jos. 5:5

the armed men. Do this for six days. Have seven priests carry trumpets of rams' horns in front of the ark. On the seventh day, march around the city seven times, with the priests blowing the trumpets. When you hear them sound a long blast on the trumpets, have the whole army give a loud shout; then the wall of the city will collapse and the army will go up, everyone straight in."

(Jos. 6:2–5)

If we are going to win our battles, we must fight them as the Lord instructs, even if the way seems crazy! The battle of Jericho was won because they *had* to depend on God for the victory. It was won by a shout not a shield. Why a shout? Derek Prince has written, "The mouth is the primary channel for releasing our spiritual weapons against Satan's kingdom."[80] They defeated Jericho with a blast from a ram's horn and a "shout," both of which obviously proceeded out of their mouths. God enabled them to conquer that which would keep them from occupying his promises.

If Christians are not destined for warfare, just heaven, then why does Paul tell us to put on the full armor of God? For us to win our struggles against the flesh and the devil,

---

[80] Derek Prince, *Spiritual Warfare,* (New Kensington, PA: Whitaker House, 1987), p. 114.

we need to follow God's battle plan—and use the armor he has given us.

> Finally, be strong in the Lord and in his mighty power. Put on the full armor of God, so that you can take your stand against the devil's schemes. For our struggle is not against flesh and blood, but against the rulers, against the authorities, against the powers of this dark world and against the spiritual forces of evil in the heavenly realms. Therefore put on the full armor of God, so that when the day of evil comes, you may be able to stand your ground, and after you have done everything, to stand. Stand firm then, with the belt of truth buckled around your waist, with the breastplate of righteousness in place, and with your feet fitted with the readiness that comes from the gospel of peace. In addition to all this, take up the shield of faith, with which you can extinguish all the flaming arrows of the evil one. Take the helmet of salvation and the sword of the Spirit, which is the word of God. And pray in the Spirit on all occasions with all kinds of prayers and requests. With this in mind, be alert and always keep on praying for all the Lord's people.
>
> (EPH. 6:10–18)

There are several specific pieces of armor that directly relate, not only to our battles, but also to the one at Jericho. Let us work our way through that passage. Verse 10 clearly warns us to do spiritual warfare in God's power, not our own. The Israelites depended on God's power to level the walls of Jericho; the arm of flesh was sorely insufficient. And us?

> For though we live in the world, we do not wage war as the world does. The weapons we fight with are not the weapons of the world. On the contrary, they have divine power to demolish strongholds. We demolish arguments and every pretension that sets itself up against the knowledge of God, and we take captive every thought to make it obedient to Christ.
>
> (2 COR. 10:3–5)

The next verse in Ephesians (6:11) warns us to put on God's armor, not man's. Our military does its best to outfit a soldier for combat, but those preparations are useless in an invisible war; only God's armor can protect us. Verse 12 reminds us this is a battle of unseen forces: God's power vs. Satan's. For the second time in this passage, one is told to put on God's armor (vv. 10, 13) if he is to stand his ground in this battle.

The armor is then delineated: (1) the belt of truth (v.

14)—one must depend on the truth of God's word not man's word. Even an excellent book on spiritual warfare is no match for the pure word of God. (2) The breastplate of righteousness (v. 14)—the breastplate covers one's heart. When doing battle, we must depend on the righteousness of Christ, not our own. (Since our account is bankrupt!) (3) Feet fitted with…the gospel of peace (v. 15)—much of our warfare will be in the field of personal evangelism. We must always be ready and willing to share our faith with others—remembering the resistance they often offer is an influence from an unseen, dark realm. (4) The shield of faith (v. 16)—we must always, always believe the gospel and the word of God have power. Satan will shoot his "flaming arrows" of doubt at us. If we don't hold on to faith and keep it in its proper position, we will fail and fall in battle. I encourage you to fill you heart and mind with as much scripture, godly literature, and Christian music as possible. Avoid shield-wrecking, doubt-causing influences of all kinds. For many of us, the answer is turning off the TV. My wife says the "off" button is the only one I have difficulty finding on the remote. Confession time: she's right (she will love seeing that in print). Next, we need (5) the helmet of salvation (v. 17), which God gives us to protect our thinking. I believe Joyce Meyer would agree with this as she has written a book on spiritual warfare entitled *Battlefield of the Mind*. This leaves only (6) the sword of the Spirit (v. 17), which is our first offensive weapon. Paul left no doubt but defined it for us—the word of God. This means using the word of God to attack the strongholds of the evil one. The perfect example of this can be found in Jesus' confrontation with the devil in the wilderness (Matt. 4:1–11; Lk. 4:1–13).

Man's Battle Plans

It is unfortunate, but the scriptures, as well as life, demonstrate this fact: Although one has received the baptism (filling) of the Holy Spirit, he can still act independently of God. Even Sprit-filled people can decide to act out of the flesh. What happens when man decides to take things into his own hands and do things his own way? Defeat. How many in a group does it take to damage the whole group? Never underestimate the power of one person for good or for evil.

When I was in high school our basketball team had a seven-foot standout named Luke Witte. After high school, Luke played for Ohio State University and later for the Cleveland Cavaliers of the NBA. While in high school, Luke led our basketball team to two great seasons. His junior year, the team went 18–0 in regular season; and during his senior year, they went 17–1. After he graduated, the team had a "mirror record," going 1–17 and

0–18 in the next two seasons. It is amazing how much *good* influence one person can have! It is also amazing how much *evil* influence one person can have.

Enter Achan.

Who is Achan? Achan is the man who took some of the spoils from Jericho and hid them in his tent (Jos. 7). Those things had been devoted to God.[81] We see this "spirit-filled" man—he had gone through the Jordan River—acted out of the flesh. Let's look at some of the problems of the flesh he faced:

Flesh problem 1: not depending on God's provision. Achan stole "a beautiful robe from Babylonia, two hundred shekels of silver and a wedge of gold weighing fifty shekels,"[82] Why would he not trust God to continue to provide for his needs? Oh yes—God had provided in the wilderness, but now the daily provision of manna had ceased![83] The land they were to conquer was to provide their needs.

So what happened? How did this one sinful event affect God's people? The people felt so confident about "their" victory over Jericho they decided to conquer the next (smaller) town, Ai.

---

[81] Jos. 6:17–18

[82] Jos. 7:21

[83] Jos. 5:12

Now Joshua sent men from Jericho to Ai, which is near Beth Aven to the east of Bethel, and told them, "Go up and spy out the region." So the men went up and spied out Ai.

When they returned to Joshua, they said, "Not all the army will have to go up against Ai. Send two or three thousand men to take it and do not weary the whole army, for only a few people live there." So about three thousand went up; but they were routed by the men of Ai, who killed about thirty-six of them. They chased the Israelites from the city gate as far as the stone quarries and struck them down on the slopes. At this the hearts of the people melted and became like water.

(Jos. 7:2–5)

They did not know there was sin in the camp. Did you notice how widely one sin affected the whole congregation? Thirty-six men died because of Achan's sin, and Israel was put to shame before their enemies.

Can you imagine how impotent the church has become because there is "sin in *our* camps"? If Achan's one sin caused the defeat at Ai and the loss of thirty-six lives, how is our sin affecting kingdom work? We can do better, fellow disciples.

Joshua, as their leader, sinned also. He did not inquire

of God—i.e., he did not pray. Therefore, they did not know what God's plans were. That leads us to…

Flesh problem 2: not depending on God's leading. They did not seek the Lord. They depended on their own physical strength rather than the Lord's spiritual power. They stopped depending on the Lord. Amazing! Even in the Promised Land…even amidst great victories in the Lord…the carnal man can spring up! We can NEVER trust in ourselves and where we are; we must ALWAYS trust in God.

What a terrible end to the Exodus story! Or is it the end?

Joshua responded to the defeat by lying on the ground and weeping. In response to his humility, God showed him the two problems in the camp. First, they eradicated the sin. After drawing lots, it was determined that Achan was the one to blame. Joshua charged him to tell the truth, and Achan confessed all. Because he stole things dedicated to God, he and his whole family were stoned (more death as a consequence of one sin). Second, they eradicated their self-reliance. They sought God's wisdom for taking the city and then went out and defeated Ai.

Conclusion

On a Monday evening, shortly after beginning the war with Iraq, I was with a group of pastors in a Pastoral Mentoring class (I was *being* mentored, not doing the mentoring). One of my fellow pastors asked something like, "How do we understand God telling the Israelites to kill every man, woman, and child and yet our soldiers are told to do their best not to kill innocent people?" I believe part of the answer lies in this chapter. Israel was an "example" to us (1 Cor. 10:6, 11). So, what example are we to receive from their actions? In spiritual warfare, you take no prisoners, you leave no survivors!

To be victorious in spiritual conflict, the disciple must follow the following precepts: (1) Warfare must be done in God's power—this was revealed at Jericho. (2) It cannot be done in man's power—this was remembered at Ai.

To do spiritual battle, you must be in the right place. For the Israelites, the right place was a plot of land we call the state of Israel. God had a long-standing promise with the nation that Canaan would one day be theirs. For us, the right place is the state of grace found only in salvation through Jesus Christ. As preparation to do battle, repentance and daily disciplines are in order. The more scripture you know, the better you can fight. "For the word of God is alive and active. Sharper than any double-edged sword, it penetrates even to dividing soul and spirit, joints and marrow; it judges the thoughts and attitudes of the heart" (Heb. 4:12).

If we want to live the victorious Christian life, we need to be (1) *continually* filled with His Spirit (last week), and (2) *consistent* in engaging in spiritual warfare (always out of the Spirit, not the flesh).

Discipleship Challenge

The challenge for every disciple in Christ is to never forget there is an invisible war being waged. Paul wrote on one occasion, "For our struggle is not against flesh and blood, but against the rulers, against the authorities, against the powers of this dark world and against the spiritual forces of evil in the heavenly realms" (Eph. 6:12). Our problem is we can't see the conflict with the eyes of flesh and therefore forget it is real. Dear disciple, IT IS REAL!

> Be alert and of sober mind. Your enemy the devil prowls around like a roaring lion looking for someone to devour. Resist him, standing firm in the faith, because you know that the family of believers throughout the world are undergoing the same kind of sufferings.
>
> (1 Pet. 5:8–9)

We need to learn *how* to fight.
We need to learn *who* to fight.
We need to learn to *spiritually* fight.
We need to fight.

❦ CONCLUSION ❧

Thank you for journeying through the events that comprise the greater Exodus story and their New Testament counterparts. Many things were discovered on this trek.

First, we came to understand the land of Egypt represents the human sin nature with which we are all born. We also discovered Pharaoh as a type to which Satan is the antitype. Likewise, we perceived that the shadow of Moses is found in substance as Jesus the Christ.

Second, we noticed that the establishment and celebration of the first Passover pointed to Jesus Christ being *our* Passover Lamb. We were challenged at this point to accept him as our Lord and Savior—our first step in discipleship. The author—through an excursus—caused us to reevaluate what tradition has taught us about the day of crucifixion in comparison to the Passover policies.

Third, the crossing of the Red Sea was perceived as a picture of Christian baptism—our second step in discipleship. In this chapter's excursus, we were challenged to set aside our traditional thinking and to take a fresh look at what the New Testament says on that subject.

Fourth, we journeyed through the wilderness with the fledgling nation and noticed a strong parallel to the *carnal Christian* spoken of in 1 Corinthians. Several areas of carnality were examined and noted as incompatible with a walk of faith—continuing sanctification is the third step of discipleship.

Fifth, a new view of the crossing of the Jordan at flood stage was presented. Rather than the historical view that that scene represents our physical death and crossing over to heaven, we found it paralleled "the baptism of the Holy Spirit." The reader was also encouraged to understand this view is more in alignment with New Testament teachings. Seeking being filled with the Holy Spirit should be the desire of every Christian, every disciple.

Finally, we came to the Promised Land, not with the hope of heaven, but with the hope of engaging in and winning victories in spiritual warfare. This should be our hope—glorifying the Father on earth. Thus we have the believers' path prefigured in the Exodus story. To one degree or another, all believers pass through these six stages—at least that is the goal. Unfortunately, many get stuck in stage four—the wilderness of carnal living.

The author would like to believe all his thoughts contained in this book are original. But alas, others have seen the gospel in the Exodus story as well. One noted author, N.T. Wright, has recently written:

> I have argued in detail elsewhere that the entire sequence of thought from Romans 4 through to Romans 8, for all the obvious change of gear around chapter 5, *indicates that Paul has the complete exodus narrative in mind,* from the initial promise to Abraham in Genesis 15 (where the 'covenant' specified the forthcoming exodus) through the crossing of the Red Sea which liberates the slaves, the arrival at Sinai and the giving of the law, the construction of the tabernacle, the wilderness wandering and the danger of going back into slavery, all the way to the final inheritance, the promised land.[84] (italics mine)

The hope is you have been as challenged in reading this work as the author was in writing it. Further, it is hoped

---

[84] N. T. Wright, *Paul and the Faithfulness of God, Parts I and II,* (Minneapolis: Fortress Press, 2013), p. 422.

you will strive to enter both the Promised Land of this life and the Heaven of the next.

May Christ be exalted. Amen.

Egypt	Passover	Red Sea	Wilderness	Jordan	Land
Bondage	*Redemption*	*Baptism*	*Carnal living*	*Spirit*	*Victory*
⇧	⇧	⇧	⇧	⇧	⇧

Figure C.1

◌ Appendix A ◌

The Exodus Throughout Scripture

The references to the Exodus story (from slavery in Egypt to the Promised Land) in the entire Bible are listed below. By this chart, one can see both the instances and their absences by book.

Genesis

15:13–14, 16
21:10^L
31:14^L
46:4
48:21
50:24–25

Exodus

3:8; 10–12, 17, 19–21
4:23
6:6–9, 11, 13, 26–27
7:4–5, 16
8:1–2; 20–21
9:1–2, 13, 17
10:3–4, 8–9, 26
11:1, 8
12:1–27 (Passover[85]),
    31–32, 37, 39, 41–42,
    43–49^P, 51
13:3–4, 4–10^P, 14, 16, 18–19
14:11

15:17^L, 26
16:1, 6, 32
17:3
18:1, 9–10
19:1, 4
20:2
22:21
23:9, 15^P
29:46
32:1, 4, 7–8, 11-12, 13^L, 23
33:1
34:9^L, 18^P, 25^P

Leviticus

11:45
18:3
19:34, 36
20:24^L
22:33
23:5–8, 34^T, 43
25:38, 42, 55
26:13, 45

---

[85] Every occurrence of the Passover is listed (even the mention of it in the Gospels) because it is the centerpiece of the remembrance of the entire Exodus story. All future references to the Passover will be superscripted with a "P." The feast of Tabernacles will be marked with a "T"; and *land* or *inheritance* will be marked with an "L."

18:2–4[L], 20[L], 28[L]

19:1[L], 8–10[L], 16[L], 23[L], 31[L], 39[L], 41[L], 48–49[L]

23:4[L]

24:28[L], 30[L], 32[L]

Judges

2:6[L], 9[L]

18:1[L]

20:6[L]

21:23–24[L]

Ruth

1 Samuel

2:27

4:8

6:6

8:8

10:1[L]

12:6, 8

15:2, 6

26:19[L]

2 Samuel

7:6, 23

14:16[L]

20:19[L]

21:3[L]

1 Kings

6:1

8:9, 16, 21, 36[L], 51, 53

9:9

12:28

2 Kings

17:7, 26

18:4

19:24

21:14[L], 15

23:21–23[P]

1 Chronicles

2:7

17:5, 21

28:8[L]

2 Chronicles

5:10

6:5, 27[L], 31[L], 38[L]

7:22

8:13[T]

20:7[L], 10, 11[L]

24:10

30:1–2^P, 5^P, 13^P, 15^P, 17–18^P, 21^P, 23^P

33:8^L

35:1^P, 6–9^P, 11^P, 13^P, 16–19^P

Ezra

2:4^T

3:4^T

6:19–22^P

9:11–12^L

Nehemiah

1:9^L

8:14–18^T

9:8^L, 9–21, 22–25^L, 35–36^L

13:2

Esther

Job

Psalms

16:3^L, 6^L

18:15

25:13^L

28:9^L

29:3, 8

33:12^L

37:3^L, 11^L, 22^L, 29^L, 34^L

41:2^L

44:2, 3^L

47:4^L

51:7[86]

60:2^L

61:5^L

66:6

68:7–10, 17

74:2^L

77:15–20

78:12–55, 62^L, 71^L

79:1^L

80:8-11

85:1^L, 9^L, 12^L

94:5^L, 14^L

95:8–11

99:6–8

103:7

105:11^L, 17–45

106:7–34

---

[86] Hyssop was used to put the blood on the doorframe at Passover.

111:4–6
114:1–8
125:3^L
135:8–11, 12^L
136:10–24
147:19

Proverbs
2:21–22^L
10:30^L

Ecclesiastes

Song of Solomon

Isaiah
1:2, 4
4:5–6
10:24, 26
11:11, 15–16
14:1–2^L
17:10
19:22
22:11
28:21
29:1
33:20

41:9
43:1, 16–17, 20–21
44:1–2, 27
48:21
50:2
51:9–10
52:44
63:11–14

Jeremiah
2:1, 6–7, 21
3:18–19^L
7:7L, 22–26
11:4–5, 7–8, 10
12:14–15
15:1
16:14
17:4, 22
23:7
24:10^L
25:5^L
30:3^L
31:32
32:20–23
34:13
35:15^L
52:27^L

Lamentations

1:4

2:6–7

5:2^L

Ezekiel

11:15^L

13:9^L

16:8

20:5–26, 34–36, 42

23:1–4, 8, 19–21, 27

28:25^L

33:24–26^L

35:15^L

36:12^L, 28^L, 38

37:12–14^L, 25^L

39:25

44:24, 28^L

45:1^L, 5–8^L, 17, 21^P, 23^P, 25^T

46:9, 11, 16–18^L

47:13–14^L, 21–2 3^L

48:29^L

Daniel

8:9^L

9:6^L, 10–11, 13, 15

11:16^L, 28, 30, 41^L

12:13^L

Hosea

1:11

2:11, 15, 23^L

8:12–13

9:3, 5, 10

11:1, 5

12:9, 13

Joel

1:2^L

2:18^L

Amos

2:10

3:1

4:10

5:2^L, 25

7:11^L, 17^L

9:7, 15^L

Obadiah

1:17^L

Jonah

Micah

2:2^{L}

6:4–5

7:15

Nahum

1:4, 15

Habakkuk

3:3–15[87]

Zephaniah

2:3^{L}, 9^{L}

3:18

Haggai

2:4^{L}, 5

Zechariah

9:16

14:16^{T}, 18^{T}, 19^{T}

Malachi

4:4

Matthew

2:15

26:2^{P}, 17–19^{P}

Mark

14:1^{P}, 12^{P}, 14^{P}, 16^{P}

15:6^{P}

Luke

2:41^{P}

9:31[88]

22:1^{P}, 7–8^{P}, 11^{P}, 13^{P}, 15^{P}

John

1:17

2:13^{P}, 23^{P}

3:14

6:2^{P}, 31–32, 49, 58

11:55^{P}

12:1^{P}

7:2^{T}

13:1^{P}

18:28^{P}, 39^{P}

19:14^{P}

---

[87] Carl E. Armerding, "Habakkuk," *The Expositor's Bible Commentary,* Vol. 7, (Grand Rapids: Zondervan, 1985), pp. 520–532.

[88] The word used for "departure" in this verse is the Greek word *exodus*.

Acts
3:22–23
7:6–7, 9–15, 17–45
12:3–4[P]
13:17–19
20:6[P]

Romans
9:17

1 Corinthians
5:7–8[P]
10:1–10

2 Corinthians
3:7, 13
8:13[T], 15

Galatians
3:19

Ephesians

Philippians

Colossians

1 Thessalonians

2 Thessalonians

1 Timothy

2 Timothy
3:8–9

Titus

Philemon

Hebrews
3:2–11, 15–19
4:2–3, 5, 7–8
8:5, 9
9:19-21
10:1, 30
11:9, 22–31, 28[P]
12:18–21, 25–26

James
2:25

1 Peter
1:19

2 Peter
2:15–16

1 John

2 John

3 John

Jude

1:5, 11

Revelation[89]

5:6, 8–9, 12–13

6:1, 3, 5, 7, 16

7:9–10, 14, 17

8:7–8, 12

9:3

11:3, 6, 8, 10, 19

12:11, 14

13:8

14:1, 4, 10

15:1, 3, 6, 8

16:2–4, 9–10, 12–13, 21

17:14

18:4, 8

19:7, 9

21:23, 27

22:1, 3 18

---

[89] Every time the words "Lamb," "plague," or an allusion to something in the Exodus story, such as "the song of Moses" will be listed

⊗ Appendix B ⊗

The Last Week of Jesus' Life

Sunday

Triumphal entry — Matthew 21:1–11; Mark 11:1–10; Luke 19:28–40; John 12:12–19

Weeping over Jerusalem — Luke 19:41–44

Monday

Cleared the Temple — Matthew 21:12–17; Mark 11:11–19; Luke 19:45–48

Cursed fig tree — Mathew 21:18–19b; Mark 11:12–14

Tuesday

Withered fig tree — Mathew 21:19c–22; Mark 11:20–26

Jesus' authority questioned — Matthew 21:23–27; Mark 11:27–33; Luke 20:1–8

Parable of the two sons — Mathew 21:28–32

Parable of the tenants — Matthew 21:33–46; Mark 12:1–12; Luke 20:9–19

Parable of the wedding feast — Matthew 22:1–14

Paying taxes to Caesar — Matthew 22:15–22; Mark 12:13–17; Luke 20:20–26

Marriage and the resurrection — Matthew 22:23–33; Mark 12:18–27; Luke 20:27–40

Greatest Commandment — Matthew 22:34–40; Mark 12:28–34

Whose son is the Christ — Matthew 22:41–46; Mark 12:35–40; Luke 20:41–47

Widow's offering — Mark 12:41–44; Luke 21:1–4

Seven woes — Matthew 23:1–39

Signs of the end — Matthew 24:1–51; Mark 13:1–37; Luke 21:5–36

Parable of the ten virgins — Matthew 25:1–13

Parable of the talents — Matthew 25:14–30

Parable of the sheep and goats — Mathew 25:31–46

Plot against Jesus — Matthew 26:1–5

Jesus anointed at Bethany — Matthew 26:6–13; Mark 14:1–9; John 12:1–8

Judas agrees to betray Jesus — Matthew 26:14–16; Mark 14:10–11; Luke 22:1–6

Wednesday

Preparation and last supper — Matthew 26:17–30; Mark 14:12–26; Luke 22:7–23; John 13:1–30

Dispute about who is the greatest — Luke 22:24–30

Jesus predicts Peter's denial — Matthew 26:31–35; Mark 14:27–31; Luke 22:31–38; John 13:31–38

Upper room discourse — John 14:1–17:26

Gethsemane — Matthew 26:36–46; Mark 14:32–42; Luke 22:39–46

Thursday

Jesus arrested — Matthew 26:47–56; Mark 14:43–52; Luke 22:47–53; John 18:1–11

Trial before the Sanhedrin — Matthew 26:57–68; Mark 14:53–65; Luke 22:66–71; John 18:12–14, 19–24

Peter's three denials — Mathew 26:69–75; Mark 14:66–72; Luke 22:54–62; John 18:15–18, 25–27

Judas hangs himself — Matthew 27:1–10

Jesus before Pilate — Matthew 27:11–26; Mark 15:1–15; Luke 23:1–25 (Herod also); John 18:28–19:16a

Jesus mocked by guards — Matthew 27:27–31; Mark 15:16–20

The crucifixion — Matthew 27:32–56; Mark 15:21–41; Luke 23:26–49; John 19:16b–37

Burial of Jesus — Matthew 27:57–61; Mark 15:42–47; Luke 23:50–56; John 19:38–42

Guards seal the tomb — Matthew 27:62–66

Friday (First day—in the tomb)

Saturday (Second day—in the tomb)

Sunday (Third day)

Resurrection — Matthew 28:1–10; Mark 16:1–8; Luke 24:1–12; John 20:1–18

Guard's report — Matthew 28:11–15

Road to Emmaus — Luke 24:13–35

Jesus appears to the disciples — Luke 24:36–49; John 20:19–30

cʒ APPENDIX C ℬ

Study Guide

A select number of discussion questions has been provided for the introduction, each chapter, and each excursus. This guide has been developed for an eleven-week study plan using the introduction, the six chapters, and the four excursuses separately. If you need a study to take a complete quarter, some chapters may be long enough to be covered in two studies. Space has been provided for the discussion leader to jot down a few questions of his/her own. If you are the group discussion leader, please remember the three kinds of questions to ask:

1. INFORMATION (Clarification) to make sure the participants understand the facts of the passage.

Use this type of question the least. They are usually close-ended questions (having only one answer) and therefore do not lead the group to discuss.

2. INTERPRETATION (Comprehension) to make sure the student understands the original meanings of a passage. Ask this type of question more frequently. These should be open-ended questions (having more than one answer, like, "What is your favorite flavor of ice cream?") which have the potential for stirring the participants to deep thought and understanding.

3. INTEGRATION (Application) to challenge the student not to just learn the material but to apply it to one's life. When the details of each topic have been thoroughly covered, ask this type of question to spur the participants to apply the passage to their lives, rather than just gaining more head knowledge. Again, these should be open-ended questions.

Introduction

1. Define the following:
   - Type
   - Shadow
   - What is the difference between them?

2. Why do you think God chose the nation of Israel to display his plan of salvation to the nations?

3. What benefits do you thinks there are in studying the scriptures through the use of types and shadows?

4. What do you think each of the following types might represent? I will give you one.
   - The Israelites as slaves in Egypt? —
   - The Passover? —
   - Crossing the Red Sea? — Christian baptism (1 Corinthians 10:2)
   - The forty-year wilderness journey? —

- Crossing the Jordan River? —
- The Promised Land? —

5. What do you hope to learn through this study of the Exodus?

6. Why do you believe God chose types and shadows to display his plan?

7. What was your reaction to Bercovitch's quote?

8. _____

   _____

9. _____

   _____

10. _____

    _____

Chapter One

1. In what ways do you see the land of Egypt representing our sin nature?

2. In what ways do you see Pharaoh acting the part of Satan?

3. How did Moses foreshadow our deliverer, the Christ?

4. What does the slavery in Egypt represent?

5. Have you ever innocently gotten yourself into a position that later became binding? What did you do to become free of that situation?

6. Can you think of any other ways Pharaoh and Satan are similar?

7. Can you think of any other ways Moses and Jesus are similar?

8. Have you ever made the choice to come out of the bondage of sin and into the forgiveness found in Jesus? If so, share briefly your conversion story. If not, why not?

9. _____

_____

10. _____

_____

11. _____

_____

Chapter Two

1. What is included in the Passover policies? (List them)

2. What is contained in the Passover promises? (List them)

3. What are the qualifications for the Passover participants? (List them)

4. What similarities do you see between the Passover lamb and Jesus Christ, the Lamb of God?

5. In what ways should we prepare for Passover today? (See 1 Corinthians 5:6–8)

6. How do we celebrate the Passover today?

7. How important was the application of the blood for the Israelites? For us?

8. Do you feel that you would qualify as a participant of the Passover meal? Of the Lord's Supper? Why or why not?

Excursus

9. According to the timing of the author, Jesus and his disciples would have either eaten the Passover one day early or they were not eating the Passover at the Last Supper. Does that make sense? (One could stand during any advent service and say, "I have looked forward to celebrating this Christmas with you.")

10. What validity (if any) did you find in the author's plea for a Thursday crucifixion? What did he share you thought was not well defended?

11. How does one bring into agreement the author's viewpoint with that of Matthew 27:62, Mark 15:42, Luke 23:54, and John 19:14?

12. If you accept a Thursday crucifixion, should you *push* this teaching on others? Should you make it a point of contention or division?

13. Have you ever personally applied the blood of the Lamb by faith?

14. _____

15. _____

16. _____

Chapter Three

1. Do you agree with the author that Paul's words in 1 Corinthians 10:1–2 speak to the institution of Christian baptism? Why or why not?

2. When do you believe the blood is applied? Why?

3. How much do each of the following mean to you?
   List them in the order of importance for you. Why
   have you chosen that order?
   — A new way of life
   — A declaration of allegiance to God
   — A declaration of allegiance to God's appointed
   leaders
   — A new identity
   — A new direction (destination)

4. If you are a member of a local church, what is your
   church's position on water baptism?

Excursus

5. Of the three headings (mode, purpose, and
   recipients), which do you struggle with the most to
   be in agreement with the author? Why?

6. Do you believe the author correctly handled the scriptures, or did he simply promote *his group's* already established doctrinal position (after asking you to set yours aside)? Why do you think that is so?

7. How do you see Christian baptism portrayed in scripture: prescriptive, descriptive, or suggestive? Why?

8. Do you hold an either/or or both/and position in interpreting scripture? Which do you think is more biblical? Why?

9. If you have never been immersed, are you willing to do so now? Why or why not?

10. _____
    _____

11. _____
    _____

12. _____

   _____

Chapter Four

1. What are the different *sins of carnality* that kept the Israelites from possessing God's best? Can you think of others not mentioned by the author?

2. Which area of carnality (grumbling, lost focus, postponed promise) has plagued your Christian walk the most? What are you doing (or going to do) to correct this?

3. Do you understand how an attitude of carnality can obstruct God's plan? How have you seen this manifested in the local church?

4. What does "eating without regard for one's personal holiness" mean?

Excursus

5. What group (or groups) came to mind as you read this excursus? What is our (the Christian's) responsibility to them?

6. How did the apostle Paul deal with idols? (1 Cor. 10:14–22; 2 Cor. 5:14–16; Eph. 5:5; 1 Thess. 5:8–10)

7. Do you believe the author was fair in his assessment of modern-day idolatry?

8. How does 1 John 5:21 apply to this study and your life?

9. _____

_____

10. _____

_____

11. _____

_____

Chapter Five

1. Of the two interpretations presented in this chapter, which seems the more plausible to you: the traditional understanding of death or the author's suggestion of baptism with the Holy Spirit? Why?

2. Which of the author's arguments for the baptism with the Holy Spirit seems strongest? Weakest? Why?
   - Crossing the Jordan was like crossing the Red Sea, a baptism of sorts.
   - Something happened to empower them.
   - Jesus' interpretation of Isaiah 44:3 in John 7:37–39.
   - Pillars of cloud and fire gone?
   - Elijah preceded Elisha?

3. Crossing the Jordan River and being baptized in the Holy Spirit have several things in common. Which do you believe is the strongest argument?
   - Have to enter into it by faith.
   - Moses did not cross the Jordan with the Israelites?

- The memorial of stone was built in the Promised Land, not the wilderness?

4. Which of the preceding list, if any, do you believe is stretching the facts?

5. Can you think of other reasons (besides ignorance, fear, and apathy) for not seeking the baptism with the Holy Spirit?

6. When you first read the phrase "baptism with the Holy Spirit," what was your reaction?

Excursus

7. What is the strongest point the author makes for his understanding the baptism with the Holy Spirit? Why do you think that?

8. What is the weakest point the author makes for his understanding the baptism with the Holy Spirit? Why do you think that?

9. Have you ever been baptized (filled) with the Holy Spirit? If so, when?

10. Having read this chapter and excursus, write out your understanding of what it means to be baptized with the Holy Spirit.

11. _____

_____

12. _____

_____

13. _____

_____

Chapter Six

1. How many books on the topic of spiritual warfare have you read? May I suggest two based on the book of Ephesians? *Lord, Is It Warfare?* by Kay Arthur and *The Few, the Humble, the Church* by a lady in my former Word Weavers' group, Stephanie Pavlantos.

2. Do you find the author's interpretation of the Promised Land as "the victorious Christian life in the midst of spiritual warfare" to be more or less encouraging than the traditional view of heaven? Why?

3. Read Matthew 4:1–11 or Luke 4:13. What can you learn from Jesus' example of using the word of God in warfare?

4. How has your local church been diminished by "sin in the camp"?

5. What will you do to be better prepared to participate in spiritual warfare?

6. _____

_____

7. _____

_____

8. _____

_____

⋖ BIBLIOGRAPHY ⋗

2019. *A rose by any other name would smell as sweet.* September 24. Accessed November 19, 2018. https://en.wikipedia.org/wiki/A_rose_by_any_other_name_would_smell_as_sweet.

Abraham, Ken. 1991. *The Disillusioned Christian: Advice for the Burned and Burned Out.* San Bernardino, California: Here's Life Publishers, Inc.

Bercovitch, Sacvan. 1975. *The Puritan Origins of the American Self.* New Haven, Connecticut: Yale University Press.

Brown, Colin, editor. 1975. *The New International Dictionary of New Testament Theology.* Vol. 1. Grand Rapids, Michigan: Zondervan.

Bunyan, John. 1980. *The Harvard Classics: The*

Pilgrim's Progress. Danbury, Connecticut: Grolier Enterprises.

Chan, Francis, and Mark Beuving. 2012. *Multiply: Disciples Making Disciples*. Colorado Springs, Colorado: David C Cook.

Estelle, Bryan D. 2018. *Echoes of Exodus: Tracing Biblical Motif*. Downers Grove, Illinois: IVP Academic.

Gaither, William J., and Gloria Gaither. 1983. *"Because He Lives."* 3054.

Henry, Matthew. n.d. *Matthew Henry's Commentary on the Whole Bible*. Vol. 5. 6 vols. McLean, Virginia: MacDonald Publishing Company.

Hoven, Victor E. 1934. *Shadow and Substance*. Bloomington, Minnesota: Bethany Press.

Johnson, Joey. 2009. *God Is Greater Than Family Mess*. Dallas, Texas: Saint Paul Press.

Keach, Benjamin. 1972. *Preaching from the Types and Metaphors of the Bible*. Grand Rapids, Michigan: Kregel Publications.

Keener, Craig S. 2013. *Acts: An Exegetical Commentary*. Vol. 2. Grand Rapids, Michigan: Baker Book House.

Laan, Ray Vander. 1996. "Introduction." In *Echoes of His Presence: Stories of the Messiah from the People of His Day*, by Ray Vander Laan, 145, 147. Colorado Springs, Colorado: Focus on the Family Publishing.

Lasor, William Sanford. 1987. "Discovering What Jewish Miqva'ot Can Tell Us About Christian Baptism." *Biblical Archaeology Review*, Jan/Feb.

Mendelson, Scott. 2014. *Five Years Ago, "Avatar" Grossed $2.7 Billion But Left No Pop Culture Footprint.* December 14. https://www.forbes.com/sites/scottmendelson/2014/12/18/avatar-became-the-highest-grossing-film-of-all-time-while-leaving-no-pop-culture-footprint/#226641d66159.

Meyer, Joyce. n.d. "Wilderness Mentality." *Joyce Meyer Ministries.* Accessed August 31, 2017. http://www.jmmindia.org/JMMSITE/jmm/ministries/Teaching%20Notes/TN25%20-%20WILDERNESS%20MENTALITY.pdf.

Nash, Donald A. 1985. *Problem Passages Probed.* Grayson, Kentucky: Witness Press.

Nathan, Rich, and Ken Wilson. 2009. *Empowered Evangelicals: Bringing Together the Best of the Evangelical and Charismatic Worlds.* Boise, Idaho: Ampelon Publishing.

2015. *Northfield United Methodist Parish Page.* January 9. Accessed July 18, 2017. https://www.facebook.com/permalink.php?id=153069421385186&story_fbid=1054872024538250.

Oden, Robert. 1996. "God and Mankind: Comparative Religions." *The Great Courses® on Tape.* (Chantilly, Virginia: The Teaching Company.

n.d. *President George W Bush and Moses Joke.* Accessed July 19, 2017. http://www.free-funny-jokes.com/george-and-moses.html.

Prince, Derek. 1987. *Spiritual Warfare.* Kensington, Pennsylvania: Whitaker House.

Proctor, Matt. 2013. *Victorious: A Devotional Study of Revelation.* Joplin, Missouri: College Press.

Silberman, Neil Asher. 1989. *Biblical Archeology Review*, March/April: 58-59.

Stennett, Samuel. n.d. *On Jordan's Stormy Banks.*

Strong, James. n.d. *Exhaustive Concordance of the Bible with Expanded Greek-Hebrew Dictionary.* Nashville, Tennessee: Regal Publishing.

Swindoll, Charles R. 1986. *Growing Deep in the Christian Life.* Portland, Oregon: Multnomah Press.

Unger, Merrill F. 1988. *The New Unger's Bible Dictionary.* Chicago, Illinois: Moody Press.

Vermes, Geza. 1997. *The Complete Dead Sea Scrolls in English.* New York, New York: Penguin Press.

Vine, W.E. 1966. *An Expository Dictionary of New Testament Words.* Old Tappan, New Jersey: Fleming H. Revell Company.

1974. *Webster's New World Dictionary.* Second Edition. Cleveland, Ohio: William Collins + World Publishing.

n.d. *What are the beliefs of Jesus only/oneness Pentecostals?* Accessed August 1, 2017. https://www.gotquestions.org/oneness-Jesus-only.html.

Witherington, Ben III. 2016. "It's About Time—Easter Time." May/June: 26.

Wright, N. T. 2013. *Paul and the Faithfulness of God, Parts I and II.* Minneapolis, Minnesota: Fortress Press.

—. 2011. *Simply Jesus: A New Vision of Who He Was, What He Did, and Why He Matters.* San Francisco, California: HarperOne.

CPSIA information can be obtained
at www.ICGtesting.com
Printed in the USA
LVHW082053011020
667583LV00004B/11